Crime and Punishment in America

REFERENCE LIBRARY CUMULATIVE INDEX

Crime and Punishment in America

REFERENCE LIBRARY CUMULATIVE INDEX

CUMULATES INDEXES FOR:
Crime and Punishment in America: Almanac
Crime and Punishment in America: Biographies
Crime and Punishment in America: Primary Sources

Sarah Hermsen, Index Coordinator

U·X·L
An imprint of Thomson Gale,
a part of The Thomson Corporation

THOMSON
GALE™

Detroit • New York • San Francisco • San Diego • New Haven, Conn. • Waterville, Maine • London • Munich

Crime and Punishment in America: Cumulative Index

Project Editor
Sarah Hermsen

Product Design
Michelle Dimercurio

Composition
Evi Seoud

Manufacturing
Rita Wimberley

Library of Congress Cataloging-in-Publication Data
Crime and punishment in America reference library : cumulative index / Sarah Hermsen, index coordinator.
    p. cm. — (Crime and punishment in America reference library)
    Cumulates indexes for: Crime and Punishment in America: Almanac, Crime and Punishment in America: Biographies, Crime and Punishment in America: Primary Sources.
ISBN 0-7876-9174-7 (pbk.)
    1. Crime—United States—History—Juvenile literature—Indexes. 2. Punishment—United States—History—Juvenile literature—Indexes. 3. Criminal justice, Administration of—United States—History—Juvenile literature—Indexes. 4. Criminals—United States—Biography—Juvenile literature—Indexes. I. Hermsen, Sarah. II. Hanes, Richard Clay, 1946–Crime and punishment in America. Almanac. III. Hanes, Richard Clay, 1946–Crime and punishment in America. Biographies. IV. Hanes, Sharon M. Crime and punishment in America. Primary sources. V. Series.
Z5703.5.U5.C73 2004
[HV6779]
016.364973—dc22
    2004017555

Crime and Punishment in America
Reference Library Cumulative Index

A1 = Crime and Punishment in America: Almanac, volume 1
A2 = Crime and Punishment in America: Almanac, volume 2
B = Crime and Punishment in America: Biographies
PS = Crime and Punishment in America: Primary Sources

A

A Christmas Carol (Dickens)
  B: 63
"A Dinner at Popular Walk"
  (Dickens)
  B: 63
A Tale of Two Cities (Dickens)
  B: 66, 67 (ill.)
Abagnale, Frank W.
  A: 1: 98–100
Abbey, Edward
  A: 1: 177–78
Abduction, *A: 2:* 364–66
  AMBER Alert system, *PS:*
  174–76, 181–82
  Internet, *PS:* 193
Abolition of capital punishment
  A: 2: 400, 402–3
  PS: 116
Abortion
  Comstock law, *PS:* 81–82
  state laws, *PS:* 84
Absolute power
  PS: 17
Academic freedom
  B: 49, 50–51

Accused
  rights of the, *PS:* 49–50, 51
  witchcraft, *PS:* 30–36, 35 (ill.)
Achille Lauro
  A: 1: 180
ACLU (American Civil Liberties
  Union)
  B: 3, 8, 50, 72
  PS: 207
Acquaintance rape
  A: 1: 71
"Act for Enrolling and Calling
  Out the National Forces"
  B: 187, 188–89
ADAM (Arrestee Drug Abuse
  Monitoring) Program
  A: 1: 141–42
Adams, Elizabeth
  B: 182
Adams, John Quincy
  B: 14–15
ADD (Attention deficit disorder)
  B: 112–13
Addams, Jane
  A: 2: 294, 295 (ill.), 343
  B: 1–9, 2 (ill.)

Bold italic type indicates set
titles. **Bold** type indicates
main *Biographies* or *Primary
Sources* entries, and their
page numbers. Illustrations
are marked by (ill.).

Addams, John Huy
  B: 3, 4
Addiction, drug
  A: 1: 141
Adjudication
  A: 2: 302
Adler, Polly
  PS: 77 (ill.)
Administrative enforcement of
    environmental law
  A: 1: 159
Advance-fee loan scams
  A: 1: 101
Adversarial system
  A: 2: 298
Advocates
  juveniles', *A: 2:* 355
  victims', *A: 2:* 240–41
Afghanistan, *A: 1:* 184–85
  Al Qaeda training camps, *PS:*
    227 (ill.)
  Operation Enduring Freedom,
    PS: 208
  opium production, *PS:* 96
  "War on Terrorism," *PS:* 186,
    203, 210
African Americans. *See* Black
    Americans
African countries
  PS: 116
Age
  crime rates, *A: 1:* 226
  juvenile justice, *A: 2:* 294,
    340, 342
  murder rates, *A: 1:* 63–64
  rape, *A: 1:* 73–74
Aggravated assault
  A: 1: 68–70
"The Aggregate Burden of
    Crime" (Anderson)
  A: 2: 412–13
Aggression and testosterone
  A: 1: 221
Aid. *See* Taxes
Aid to Families with Dependent
    Children
  A: 2: 362
Aime, Laurie
  B: 35
Air India Boeing 747
  A: 1: 184
Air quality standards
  A: 1: 152–53

Al Qaeda, *A: 1:* 171–72, 174,
    181, 184
  Afghanistan, *PS:* 203, 210
  arrests, *PS:* 208
  current threat, *PS:* 215–16, 230
  hideouts, *PS:* 215 (ill.)
  intelligence gathering, *PS:* 204
  training camps, *PS:* 227 (ill.)
"Al Qaeda Training Manual"
  PS: **214–32**
Alabama
  PS: 117
Alabama, Norris v.
  B: 165, 168
Alabama, Powell v.
  B: 166
Alabama Supreme Court
  B: 166
Alaska
  A: 1: 149 (ill.), 150, 163–65,
    164 (ill.)
Alcatraz
  A: 1: 47; *2:* 308
Alcohol. *See* Prohibition
Alcohol and crime
  A: 1: 137–40, 224
Alcoholism
  PS: 71
ALF (Animal Liberation Front)
  A: 1: 178
Alfred P. Murrah Federal Building
  A: 1: 177 (ill.)
Aliens Act of 1902
  B: 83
All the Year Round
  B: 66, 68
Allen, E. J. *See* Pinkerton, Allan
Ally McBeal (TV show)
  A: 2: 447
Almighty Latin King Nation
  A: 1: 127
Alternate education programs
  A: 2: 390–91
Altgeld, John Peter
  B: 47, 48
Alzheimer's disease patients
  PS: 182
AMBER Alert. *See also* PROTECT
    Act of 2003
  A: 2: 365
  PS: 157 (ill.), 159, 174
**"Amendments to the Constitu-
    tion"**
  PS: **46–55**

America. *See* United States
American Association of Retired
    Persons
  A: 1: 102
American Bar Association
  A: 2: 442
American bond market
  B: 20
American Civil Liberties Union
    (ACLU)
  B: 3, 8, 50, 72
  PS: 207
American Civil War
  B: 158, 159, 187, 188–89
American Communist Party
  B: 92, 110, 166
American Mafia. *See also* Orga-
    nized crime
  B: 108–9
  PS: 148 (ill.), 153 (ill.),
    153–54
American Media building
  A: 1: 183 (ill.)
American Notes (Dickens)
  B: 65
  PS: **56–65**
American Online (AOL)
  PS: 182–83
American penitentiary systems.
    See Prison reform
American Revolution. *See* Revo-
    lutionary War
American Society for the Pre-
    vention of Cruelty to Ani-
    mals
  A: 2: 366
American Sugar Refining Com-
    pany
  PS: 140
American Telephone and Tele-
    graph (AT&T)
  PS: 143
American Tobacco
  PS: 141
Amnesty Association
  B: 45
Amnesty International
  A: 1: 173
Anarchists
  B: 78–86, 81 (ill.)
Anderson, David A.
  A: 2: 412
Anglican Church. *See* Church of
    England

Animal Liberation Front (ALF)
   A: 1: 178
Animals
   animal rights terrorist groups,
      A: 1: 178
   Endangered Species Act, A: 1:
      154
   prisoners and, A: 2: 312
Anonymity and cyber crime
   A: 1: 207–8
Answered Prayers (Capote)
   B: 43
Anthony, Susan B.
   B: 136–37, 137 (ill.)
Anthrax
   A: 1: 183
Antiabortion activists
   A: 1: 176
Anti-Drug Abuse Acts
   PS: 95
Anti-Evolution Law, Tennessee's
   B: 49, 50–51
Anti-Federalists
   PS: 47
Anti-Saloon League
   PS: 98, 99 (ill.)
Antiterrorism Assistance program
   PS: 210
Antitrust Division, FBI
   A: 1: 109
Antitrust legislation
   PS: 136–41
Antiwar riots
   A: 2: 257
Apartments
   PS: 220–21
APEC (Asia Pacific Economic
      Cooperation Group)
   PS: 205
Appeals
   juveniles, A: 2: 353
   military justice, A: 2: 325,
      333–34
Appellate courts
   A: 2: 290, 293
Apprehension
   A: 2: 304
Arab-Palestinian terrorism
   organizations, A: 1: 170
   suicide bombers, A: 1: 182–83
Arbuckle, Roscoe "Fatty"
   A: 2: 439–40
Archer Daniels Midland Company
   A: 1: 109

Arizona
   capital punishment, PS: 116
Arizona, Miranda v.
   B: 147, 150, 151
Arkansas, Epperson v.
   B: 51
Armed robbery
   A: 1: 66
Arraignment
   A: 2: 301
Arrestee Drug Abuse Monitoring
      (ADAM) Program
   A: 1: 141–42
Arrests
   black Americans, A: 2: 423
   juvenile delinquents, A: 2:
      341 (ill.)
   race/ethnicity, A: 2: 430–32
Arsenals
   PS: 225
Arson. See also Fire setting
   A: 1: 75, 88–90, 89 (ill.)
Articles of Confederation
   A: 2: 206
Aryan Republican Army
   A: 1: 67 (ill.)
Ashcroft, John
   A: 1: 194 (ill.)
   PS: 204, 220 (ill.)
Ashurst-Summers Act
   A: 1: 48–49
Asia Pacific Economic Coopera-
      tion Group (APEC)
   PS: 205
Asian Americans
   A: 2: 431
Assassinations
   A: 1: 179–80
Assaults
   A: 1: 68–70, 137
Assembly, right to peaceable
   PS: 49
Assets, terrorists'
   PS: 205, 208
Association Against the Prohibi-
      tion Amendment
   PS: 100
AT&T (American Telephone and
      Telegraph)
   PS: 143
Atherton, Edwin
   B: 181
Atmore Prison
   PS: 171

At-Risk Child Care program
   A: 2: 362
Attempted forcible entry
   A: 1: 78
Attention deficit disorder (ADD)
   B: 112–13
Attica Correctional Facility
   A: 2: 309
Attorney General, U.S.
   PS: 177, 180
Attorneys, A: 2: 299 (ill.), 350
      (ill.), 443 (ill.). See also Pros-
      ecutors
   Bailey, F. Lee, B: 174–75
   colonial period, A: 1: 12
   court-martials, A: 2: 331–32
   Darrow, Clarence, B: 45–52
   defense attorneys, A: 2: 298–99
   Frankfurter, Felix, B: 71–72
   Leibowitz, Samuel, B: 165,
      165 (ill.)
   Lockwood, Belva Ann, B:
      127–33
   Mansfield, Arabella, B: 134–40
   public defenders, A: 2: 299,
      300 (ill.)
   right to, A: 1: 27; 2: 350 (ill.)
Auburn plan of corrections
   PS: 56, 58
Auburn Prison
   A: 1: 32 (ill.), 32–33
   B: 14
Auburn System
   B: 64
Aum Shinrikyo
   A: 1: 173, 182
Australia
   PS: 116
Authors. See Writers
Automobile accident insurance
      fraud
   A: 1: 102
Automobile theft
   B: 148

B

Babb, Belle Aurelia. See Mans-
      field, Arabella
Baby boom
   A: 1: 63–64
BAC (breath alcohol contraction)
   A: 1: 139–40

Bail
 A: 2: 301
Bailey, F. Lee
 B: 174–75, 175 (ill.)
Baird, Nancy
 B: 35
Bakers
 PS: 25
Balance of power
 A: 2: 284
Balch, Lewis
 PS: 115
Ball, Brenda Carol
 B: 35
Bandello, Rico (character)
 PS: 151
Bank fraud
 A: 1: 97–100
Bank robbery
 A: 1: 67 (ill.)
Bankruptcy fraud
 A: 1: 103
Bases of terrorist operations
 PS: 220–21
Bates, Ruby
 B: 164, 167
 PS: 162, 163
"The Battered Child Syndrome"
 A: 2: 367
Bay Ship Management, Inc.
 A: 1: 96–97
Beaumont, Gustave de
 A: 1: 31
 B: 10–16
Bedlam
 B: 144 (ill.), 145
Behavioral crime scene analysis
 B: 123
Behavioral problems
 A: 2: 387–88
Behavioral Science Unit (BSU)
 B: 123
Benevolence International Foundation
 PS: 205
Berkman, Alexander
 B: 81–82, 83
Berkowitz, David
 A: 2: 234
BIA (Bureau of Indian Affairs)
 A: 2: 335 (ill.), 336, 338
Bid rigging
 PS: 144

"Big Bill." *See* Haywood, William Dudley
Biker gangs
 A: 1: 122, 123 (ill.)
Bill of Rights, A: 1: 27–28; 2: 231–32, 328–29; PS: 43 (ill.)
 adoption of, PS: 54
 criminal justice system, influence on the, PS: 51
 Madison, James, PS: 44, 47–48
Bin Laden, Osama
 A: 1: 171–72, 172 (ill.), 174, 184
 PS: 205, 210, 212, 230
Biological hazards
 A: 1: 155
Biological terrorism
 A: 1: 182–83
Bird, Alice
 B: 135
Birth control
 PS: 79, 80–86
Black Americans
 arrest statistics, A: 2: 423
 "Black Codes," A: 1: 5, 36; 2: 421
 capital punishment, A: 2: 403, 428–29
 Civil Rights Movement, A: 2: 256–57
 crime and, A: 2: 416–17, 422–24
 Crips and Bloods, A: 1: 123–26, 124 (ill.)
 incarceration rates, A: 2: 429
 Jim Crow laws, A: 2: 422
 juvenile crime, A: 2: 345
 legal protections, A: 1: 36
 police, A: 1: 36
 racial profiling, A: 2: 425–27
 Scottsboro Boys, PS: 161 (ill.)
 "Scottsboro Case Goes to the Jury," excerpt from, PS: 166–69
 Scottsboro trial, overview of the, PS: 160–65
 segregation, PS: 156, 158
 "three strikes" laws, A: 2: 433
 victims, A: 2: 423–24
"Black Codes"
 A: 1: 5, 36; 2: 421
Black, Cofer
 PS: 201

Black Panther Party
 A: 1: 125
Blasphemy
 A: 1: 15–16
Blodget, Henry
 A: 1: 107
Bloods and Crips
 A: 1: 123–26, 124 (ill.), 128–29
"Blue laws"
 PS: 76–77
Bly, Nellie
 B: 82
"Bobbies"
 A: 2: 249
Boesky, Ivan
 B: 17–23, 18 (ill.)
Bogus stock
 A: 1: 201
BOI (Bureau of Investigation). *See also* Federal Bureau of Investigation (FBI)
 A: 1: 41; 2: 255
Bombings
 bomb response units, A: 2: 273–74
 Oklahoma City bombing, A: 1: 51, 176, 177 (ill.), 181
 terrorist, A: 1: 51, 180–83
 Weathermen, A: 1: 174
Bombs
 communism and, B: 90
 Kaczynski, Ted and, B: 97, 99–101, 102
 Kinkel, Kip and, B: 113, 116, 118
Bonaparte, Napoleon
 A: 2: 249
Bond ratings
 B: 20
Bond system
 A: 1: 18
Boot camp prisons
 A: 2: 310, 410 (ill.)
Booth, John Wilkes
 A: 2: 280
Booth, Maude Ballington
 A: 2: 398
Bootlegging
 A: 1: 118
 B: 55, 56, 179
 PS: 69, 99, 100, 150
Borden, Abby Durfee
 B: 24–26, 29

Borden, Andrew Jackson
  B: 24–26, 27, 27 (ill.), 29
Borden, Lizzie
  B: 24–30, 25 (ill.)
Boston Archdiocese
  A: 2: 371–73
Boston police strike
  A: 2: 252
Bourbon dynasty
  B: 11
Bow Street Runners
  A: 2: 266–67
Bowen, Seabury
  B: 26, 29
Bowling for Columbine (film)
  A: 2: 385
Bowman, Margaret
  B: 35, 37, 37 (ill.)
Boys Working Reserve
  B: 54
"Boz." *See* Dickens, Charles
Brady Act
  A: 1: 199
Brady Handgun Violence Protec-
    tion Act of 1993
  B: 115
Brattle, Thomas
  PS: 39–40
Bratton, William
  A: 1: 215
Breakfast at Tiffany's (Capote)
  B: 41
Breaking and entering
  A: 1: 79
Breath alcohol contraction
    (BAC)
  A: 1: 139–40
Breed v. Jones
  A: 2: 347
Bridges, R. R.
  B: 164, 165
  PS: 165, 166, 167
British loyalists
  A: 1: 25
Broken Windows theory of
    crime
  A: 1: 214–15; *2:* 262
Brown, John
  B: 158, 159
Brown, William H.
  A: 2: 444
Bryan, William Jennings
  B: 50, 51

Bryant, Kobe
  A: 2: 447–48
BSU (Behavioral Science Unit)
  B: 123
Buford
  B: 84, 91
Bullying
  A: 2: 382, 388
Bundy, Ted
  A: 1: 65, 65 (ill.)
  B: 31–38, 32 (ill.)
Bureau of Corporations
  PS: 140
Bureau of Federal Prisons
  A: 1: 47
Bureau of Indian Affairs (BIA)
  A: 2: 335 (ill.), 336, 338
Bureau of Internal Revenue
  B: 181
Bureau of Investigation (BOI).
    See also Federal Bureau of
    Investigation (FBI)
  A: 1: 41; *2:* 255
Bureau of Justice Statistics
  A: 2: 413
Burglary
  A: 1: 75, 78–81
  B: 36, 148
Burns National Detective
    Agency
  A: 2: 252
Burns, William J.
  A: 2: 252
Burr, Aaron
  A: 2: 439
Busby, Marcia. *See* Stanford,
    Sally
Bush, George W., *A: 1:* 184–85;
    2: 311 (ill.)
  Homeland Security, Depart-
    ment of, *PS:* 186
  Iraq, attack of, *PS:* 211
  PROTECT Act, signing of the,
    PS: 173, 174 (ill.)
  USA Patriot Act, *PS:* 206
  "War on Terrorism," *PS:* 184,
    209, 210
Bush, Jeb
  A: 2: 407
Business records
  PS: 206, 207
Businesses
  organized crime, *A: 1:* 115
  theft of equipment, *A: 1:* 82

C

Cable news
  A: 2: 444, 450
Cadillacs
  A: 1: 163
California, *PS:* 116
  "three strikes" laws, *A: 2:* 433
  victims' compensation pro-
    gram, *A: 2:* 234–35
Callahan, William W.
  PS: 163, 164, 166, 169
Callaway, Robbie
  PS: 175
Calley, William
  A: 2: 329
Cameras in the courtroom
  A: 2: 442–44, 449–50
Campaign strategy
  B: 106–7
Campbell, Caryn
  B: 35
Canada, *A: 1:* 145–46
  AMBER Alert programs, *PS:*
    182
  capital punishment, abolition
    of, *PS:* 116
Cannon, Dyan
  B: 183
Capital punishment. *See also*
    Death penalty; Death row;
    Executions
  abolition of, *A: 1:* 31
  African Americans, *PS:* 172
  colonial period, *A: 1:* 16–17;
    2: 400–1
  as cruel and unusual punish-
    ment, *A: 1:* 29; *PS:* 103, 105
  Dickens, Charles, beliefs of,
    PS: 64
  electrocution, development
    of, *PS:* 105
  exclusions, *A: 2:* 403–4
  federal capital crimes, *A: 2:*
    403, 405
  Kemmler, William, *PS:*
    108–15
  morality of, *A: 2:* 401
  New York State, *PS:* 115–16
  "The Plea of Clarence Dar-
    row," *PS:* 122–28
  race/ethnicity, *A: 2:* 428–29
  Scottsboro Boys, sentences of
    the, *PS:* 163

sentencing, *A: 2:* 404–5
statistics, *A: 2:* 400
Capone, Al
    A: 1: 118 (ill.); *2:* 254
    PS: 150, 151
Capote, Joseph Garcia
    B: 40
Capote, Truman
    A: 2: 446
    B: **39–44**, 40 (ill.)
Car alarms
    A: 1: 87
Car theft
    B: 148
Carneal, Michael
    A: 2: 383
Carrier, Sarah
    PS: 40
Carson, Joanne
    B: 44
Carson, Rachel
    A: 1: 148
Carter, Lester
    PS: 167
Casinos
    A: 1: 117
Catholic Church
    capital punishment, *A: 2:* 401
    child sexual abuse, *A: 2:* 369–73
    incarceration, *A: 2:* 393 (ill.),
        394
Causes of crime, *PS:* 70–71, 74
    aging and crime trends, *A: 1:*
        226
    Broken Windows theory of
        crime, *A: 1:* 214–15
    criminology, field of, *A: 1:*
        209
    drugs and alcohol, *A: 1:* 224
    education, *A: 1:* 222
    employment, low-wage, *A: 1:*
        222
    factors, *A: 1:* 209, 211
    family relationships, *A: 1:*
        218–19
    firearms, access to, *A: 1:* 224
    hate crimes, *A: 2:* 434–35
    heredity and brain activity, *A:*
        1: 219–21
    hormones, *A: 1:* 221–22
    income and education explana-
        tions, *A: 1:* 214–15
    Internet information, access
        to, *A: 1:* 224–25

juvenile crime, *A: 2:* 355
minority crime rates, *A: 2:*
    435
nineteenth century explana-
    tions, *A: 1:* 211–12
peer influence, *A: 1:* 222–23
physical abnormalities expla-
    nations, *A: 1:* 212
psychological disorders expla-
    nations, *A: 1:* 213
school violence, *A: 2:* 387–89
social and economic explana-
    tions, *A: 1:* 213–14
white-collar crime, *A: 1:*
    216–17
Caverly, John R.
    PS: 128–29
CCIPS (Computer Criminal In-
    tellectual Property Section)
    A: 1: 207
    PS: 198–99
Cells, prison
    PS: 60
Cellucci, Paul
    A: 2: 375 (ill.)
Central Intelligence Agency
    (CIA)
    B: 93
Centre Street Magistrates Court
    A: 1: 13 (ill.)
Changeable message signs
    PS: 180
Chaplains, prison
    A: 2: 396–98, 397 (ill.)
Charles I
    PS: 13, 17
Charles X, King of France
    B: 11
Charter of Forest
    PS: 14
Charters
    A: 1: 3, 5
Chartists
    B: 155–56
Chattanooga News
    B: 106
Check fraud
    A: 1: 97–99, 100 (ill.)
Chem-Bio Sciences Unit, FBI
    A: 2: 276
Chemical Specialties
    A: 1: 166
Chemical terrorism
    A: 1: 182

Chemistry departments
    A: 2: 270–71, 271 (ill.)
Chernobyl nuclear power plant
    accident
    A: 1: 150
Chernyshevsky, Nikolay
    B: 80
Cherry Hill Prison
    B: 14, 65
Chicago, Illinois
    Chicago Outfit, *A: 1:* 117, 127
    riots, *A: 2:* 257, 258 (ill.)
    street gangs, *A: 1:* 127–28
"Chicago School" of thought
    A: 1: 213–14
Chicago Tribune
    B: 58 (ill.), 59
Child abuse
    A: 1: 69–70, 218–19, 219 (ill.);
        2: 354–55, 366–68, 367 (ill.)
Child Abuse Prevention and
    Treatment Act
    A: 2: 367
Child Abuse Prevention Month
    PS: 183
Child custody
    A: 2: 364, 373–74
Child development
    A: 2: 360–61
Child Health Act
    PS: 84
Child labor
    A: 2: 359 (ill.), 362–63, 363
        (ill.)
Child Online Protection Act
    (COPA)
    A: 1: 136; *2:* 376
    PS: 86
Child pornography
    A: 1: 55, 135–36
Child protective services
    A: 2: 368–69
Child Savers Movement
    A: 2: 343
Child sexual abuse
    A: 1: 70; *2:* 366, 369–73
Child support
    A: 2: 373–74, 375 (ill.)
Childcare
    A: 2: 361–62
Children. *See also* PROTECT Act
    of 2003
    attitudes about, *A: 2:* 360–61
    crimes against, *PS:* 158–59

Children's Defense Fund
  A: 2: 370
China
  A: 2: 266
  PS: 116
Choice of crime
  A: 1: 216–17
"Chop shops"
  A: 1: 86
Christian Patriots
  A: 1: 173
Christianity
  A: 2: 394, 403
Christie, Agatha
  A: 2: 445
Chronic arsons
  A: 1: 88–89
Church attendance
  PS: 22–23
Church of England
  PS: 17–18
CIA (Central Intelligence
  Agency)
  B: 93
Cigarettes
  PS: 94–95
Circuit Court of Appeals Act
  of 1891
  B: 75
Circuit courts
  A: 2: 287
  B: 74
CITAC. See Computer Investiga-
  tions and Threat Assess-
  ment Center, FBI
Cities
  inner-city schools, A: 2:
    380–81
  motor vehicle theft rates, A:
    1: 86, 88
  professional police, A: 2:
    249–50
  robbery, A: 1: 67
  urban decay, A: 2: 414 (ill.)
Citizen policing
  A: 1: 53–54
Citizenship
  A: 1: 36
Civic responsibility
  B: 6–7
Civil disobedience
  A: 2: 257, 424
Civil liberties
  Bill of Rights, A: 1: 27–28

juveniles, A: 2: 346–47
Madison, James, PS: 47–48
Magna Carta, PS: 3, 5, 8, 13
policing, A: 2: 259–60
Civil proceedings
  A: 1: 159
Civil Rights Movement
  A: 2: 257, 424
  B: 95
Civil suits. See Lawsuits
Civil War. See also American
  Civil War
  A: 1: 36; 2: 250, 326
Claims padding, insurance
  A: 1: 102
Clarence Darrow Death Penalty
  Defense College
  B: 45
Clayton Antitrust Act
  PS: 141
Clean Air Act
  A: 1: 152–53
Clean Water Act
  A: 1: 153–54
Cleckley, Herve
  A: 1: 213
Cleveland Press
  B: 174
Clifford, Mary
  A: 1: 152
Clinical Pastoral Education
  A: 2: 397
"The Club"
  A: 1: 87 (ill.)
Clutter family murder
  B: 41–42, 43
Coalition forces
  PS: 203, 208
Cocaine
  A: 1: 142–43
  PS: 88–94
Cochran, Johnnie
  A: 2: 449
Code of Judicial Conduct
  (American Bar Association)
  A: 2: 442
Codes of ethics
  A: 2: 255, 394
CODIS Unit
  A: 2: 276–77
Coke, Sir Edward
  PS: 13
Cold War
  B: 87–88, 109

Collection of unlawful debts
  PS: 150
Colonial period
  "Blue laws," PS: 76–77
  capital punishment, A: 2:
    400–1; PS: 103
  colonists, PS: 21 (ill.)
  courts, A: 1: 8–12; 2: 286
  criminal justice, PS: 42
  criminal law, A: 1: 14–16
  English control over colonists,
    A: 1: 23–25
  English legal system com-
    pared to Colonial system,
    A: 1: 8–9
  factors affecting the law, A: 1:
    6–8
  freedom of colonists, A: 1: 23
  kidnapping, A: 2: 363–64
  Good, Sarah, PS: 34–39
  "Lawes Divine, Morall and
    Martiall," PS: 17–26
  legal process, A: 1: 12–13
  magistrates, A: 1: 11–12
  original thirteen American
    colonies, A: 1: 5 (ill.)
  policing, A: 2: 246–48
  punishment, A: 2: 392, 395
  settlement, A: 1: 3–6
  witch-hunts, PS: 29–36, 33
    (ill.), 35 (ill.)
Colonial Pipeline Company
  A: 1: 166
Columbine High School
  A: 2: 379 (ill.), 382, 384–86,
    386 (ill.), 387 (ill.)
Columbine Massacre
  B: 114–15
Commanders
  A: 2: 326–27
Commerce and Labor, Depart-
  ment of
  PS: 140
Commission, American Mafia
  A: 1: 119, 120
Commission on Law Observance
  and Enforcement
  PS: 67–75
Common-law marriage
  B: 153
Communications Decency Act
  of 1996
  A: 1: 136; 2: 376
  PS: 86

Communications, terrorists'
    PS: 222–23
Communism
    American Civil Liberties
        Union and, B: 72
    Goldman, Emma and, B:
        84–86
    Hoover, J. Edgar and, B: 88,
        90–92, 95
Communist Party, American. See
    American Communist Party
Community crime prevention.
    See also Neighborhood
    Watch
    A: 1: 54–55; 2: 261 (ill.), 262,
        413–15
Community Facilities Act
    A: 2: 361
Community notification
    A: 2: 364–65
    PS: 182
Community service
    A: 2: 317 (ill.), 352 (ill.)
Community-based corrections
    development of, A: 2: 315–17
    halfway houses, A: 2: 320
    house arrest and electronic
        monitoring, A: 2: 318–19
    Intensive Probation Supervi-
        sion (IPS), A: 2: 317–18
    juvenile justice programs, A:
        2: 347
    work release programs, A: 2:
        320
Compensation
    A: 2: 234–35
Competition, business
    PS: 133, 134, 136–37, 144
Comprehensive Drug Abuse Pre-
    vention and Control Act
    PS: 95
Comprehensive Environmental
    Response, Compensation,
    and Liability Act
    A: 1: 156–57
Computer Analysis and Re-
    sponse Team, FBI
    A: 2: 279
Computer crime squads
    PS: 194
Computer Criminal Intellectual
    Property Section (CCIPS)
    A: 1: 207
    PS: 198–99

Computer Fraud and Abuse Act
    A: 1: 54
Computer Investigations and
    Threat Assessment Center,
    FBI
    PS: 190, 194–95
Computer technology. See also
    Cyber crime; Internet
    as criminal tool, A: 1: 193–95
    law enforcement use of, PS:
        192
    search warrants, PS: 207
    victim and witness security,
        A: 2: 239–40
Comstock, Anthony
    PS: 81, 81 (ill.)
Comstock Law
    B: 179
    PS: 80–87
Confessions, A: 1: 12, 13
    Leopold and Loeb, PS: 120–21
    Miranda, Ernest and, B:
        149–50, 151, 152–53
    witches, PS: 31, 41
Congress. See also U.S. Congress
    A: 1: 26
    PS: 52–53
Conrad, Earl
    PS: 171
Conscription Act of 1863
    B: 187, 188–89
Conspiracy
    Racketeer Influenced and Cor-
        rupt Organizations (RICO)
        Act, PS: 151
    Sherman Antitrust Act, PS:
        138
Constables
    A: 2: 246–47
Constitution, U.S.
    "Amendments to the Consti-
        tution" (Madison), PS:
        48–53
    balance of power, A: 2: 284
    courts, A: 2: 286–87
    ethics and, A: 2: 394
    freedom of religion, A: 2: 396
    limitations of federal govern-
        ment power, PS: 42, 44,
        51–53
    Madison, James, PS: 47–48
    military matters, A: 2: 324–25
    police powers, limitations on,
        A: 2: 248

ratification of, A: 1: 25
U.S. Supreme Court, A: 1: 26
Constitutional Convention
    PS: 47
Construction debris, dumping
    of
    A: 1: 162
Continental Congress
    A: 1: 25; 2: 324
Contraceptives. See Birth control
Contracted killings
    B: 158–59
Cooks
    PS: 25
COPA (Child Online Protection
    Act)
    A: 1: 136; 2: 376
Copies of the Magna Carta
    PS: 14–15
"Cops"
    B: 185
Copyright
    A: 1: 55–56, 194–95, 202
    B: 63–64
Coroners
    A: 1: 14
Corporate raiding
    B: 20
Corporations
    American Notes (Dickens), PS:
        44
    environmental crime, A: 1:
        162–66
    fraud, A: 1: 107–9
    white-collar crime, A: 1:
        52–53
Corrections. See also
    Community-based correc-
    tions; Prisons
    boot camp prisons, A: 2: 310,
        410 (ill.)
    death row, A: 2: 313–14
    incarceration, A: 2: 308–11
    parole, A: 2: 314–15
    Philadelphia plan, PS: 56–63
    probation, A: 2: 306–8
Corrections Corporation of
    America
    A: 2: 310
Corruption, police
    A: 2: 251
    PS: 73, 74, 75
Cortisol
    A: 1: 221–22

Cosa Nostra. *See also* Organized crime
B: 108–9
Costello, Frank
A: 1: 117
Costs of crime, *PS:* 74
annual, *A: 2:* 411
community crime prevention efforts, *A: 2:* 413–15
estimation methods, *A: 2:* 411–12
intangible costs, *A: 2:* 409
losses, *A: 2:* 409
prison construction, *A: 2:* 311
statistics, *A: 2:* 412–13
studies, *A: 2:* 411
Counterfeiting
A: 1: 35, 98, 100 (ill.)
B: 156
Counterterrorism, *A: 1:* 185–89, 187 (ill.); *2:* 253, 417. *See also* "Patterns of Global Terrorism—2002"
international action, *PS:* 186
summary of post 9/11 measures, *PS:* 201–2
USA Patriot Act, *PS:* 206–7
Counterterrorism and Forensic Science Research Unit, FBI
A: 2: 277
Court reporter
A: 2: 293 (ill.)
Court TV
A: 2: 450
Court-appointed defense lawyers
A: 2: 299, 300 (ill.)
Court-martials
A: 2: 326, 329–33, 330 (ill.)
Courtney, Robert R.
A: 1: 96
Courts, *B:* 5, 130. *See also* Federal courts; State courts; Trials; specific courts
colonial period, *A: 1:* 8–12
development of, *A: 2:* 284–86
ethics, *A: 2:* 394
policing guidelines, *A: 2:* 246
tribal justice system, *A: 2:* 335
Courts of Criminal Appeals
A: 2: 333–34
Covert information gathering
PS: 226–28
Cover-up, Catholic Church
A: 2: 373

Cowin, Jonathan
PS: 35
Crack cocaine
A: 1: 142–43, 223 (ill.); *2:* 431–32
Cracking Cases (Lee)
B: 125
Crawford, Rich
A: 2: 307 (ill.)
Credit cards
fraud, *A: 1:* 196–97
loss protection scams, *A: 1:* 101
theft, *A: 1:* 82
Crime Classification Manual (Ressler, et al.)
B: 123
Crime Commission on Law Enforcement and the Administration of Justice
A: 2: 257
Crime commissions
PS: 67–75
Crime Control Act
A: 2: 238
Crime Control and Safe Street Act
A: 1: 53; *2:* 259
Crime families. *See also* Organized crime
PS: 148 (ill.), 153 (ill.), 153–54
Crime: Its Causes and Remedies (Lombroso)
A: 1: 212
Crime laboratories. *See also* Federal Bureau of Investigation (FBI)
chemistry departments, *A: 2:* 270–71, 271 (ill.)
creation of, *A: 2:* 267–68
DNA, *A: 2:* 272–73, 273 (ill.)
explosives, *A: 2:* 273–74
fingerprints, *A: 2:* 269
firearm and toolmark identification, *A: 2:* 268, 269 (ill.)
trace evidence, *A: 2:* 272 (ill.)
Crime prevention. *See* Prevention of crime
Crime rates
fall in, *A: 2:* 262, 378
juvenile crime, *A: 2:* 344–45, 348, 356
late nineteenth and early twentieth century, *A: 1:* 37

motor vehicle theft, *A: 1:* 86, 88
Native Americans, *A: 2:* 336–39, 422
rise in, *A: 1:* 53
twentieth century, *A: 1:* 41
violent crime, *A: 1:* 57
Crime scene recreation
A: 2: 279
Crime scenes
B: 124
Crime spree
A: 2: 253–54
Crime statistics
PS: 70, 74
Crime syndicates
A: 1: 119, 128–29
Crimes. *See also* specific crimes
true, *B:* 42–43
vices or, *B:* 178–79
white-collar, *B:* 17–23
Crimes Act
A: 1: 26
Criminal defense
B: 143, 145
Criminal investigative analysis
B: 123
Criminal justice system
Magna Carta as cornerstone of, *PS:* 3, 5, 8, 13
racism, *PS:* 158
reform, *B:* 72–77
Criminal laws. *See also* Federal crimes
colonial period, *A: 1:* 14–16
discriminatory, *A: 2:* 427
states, *A: 1:* 25
Criminal personality profiling
B: 123
Criminal proceedings
A: 1: 159–60
Criminal profiling
B: 123
Criminal prosecutors. *See* Prosecutors
Criminalistics
B: 122
Criminology
A: 1: 45, 209
Crips and Bloods
A: 1: 123–26, 124 (ill.), 128–29
Crist, Buckley
B: 100–1

Cruel and unusual punishment
   capital punishment, *A: 2:* 404
   Eighth Amendment, *A: 1:* 28
   electrocution as, *PS:* 106–7
   execution methods, *A: 2:* 406
   hanging as, *PS:* 103, 105
   sentences for drug offenses,
     PS: 96
   solitary confinement, *PS:* 44,
     51, 56–57
CSI (TV show)
   A: 2: 447
Cunningham, Julie
   B: 35
Cursing
   PS: 23
Customer allocation schemes
   PS: 144
Customs Service, U.S.
   A: 2: 253
Cyber crime, *PS:* 188–90,
   191–99. *See also* Computer
   technology
   child pornography, *A: 1:*
     197–98
   cyberstalking, *A: 1:* 204
   firearm sales, *A: 1:* 199
   intellectual property theft, *A:*
     1: 202–5
   international jurisdiction, *A:*
     1: 206–7
   Internet fraud, *A: 1:* 195–97
   investigations, *A: 1:* 193
   law enforcement, *A: 1:* 205–8
   most feared Internet crimes,
     A: 1: 192 (ill.)
   online gambling, *A: 1:*
     199–200
   organized crime, *A: 1:* 129
   prescription drug sales, *A: 1:*
     198–99
   securities fraud, *A: 1:* 106–7,
     201–2
   types, *A: 1:* 54–55
Cyber Investigations Unit, FBI
   A: 1: 207
   PS: 198

D

The Daily News
   B: 65–66
   PS: 63

Dale, Sir Thomas
   PS: 20
Daniels, C. W.
   PS: 112
Daniels, Deborah J.
   PS: 181
Dar es Salaam, Tanzania
   A: 1: 181
DARE (Drug Abuse Resistance
   Education)
   A: 2: 262
DaRonch, Carol
   B: 35, 36
Darrow, Clarence
   B: **45–52**, 46 (ill.), 48 (ill.), 84
   PS: 121 (ill.), **121–30**, 127
     (ill.), 130
Darwin, Charles
   B: 49
Database, fingerprint
   A: 2: 269
David Copperfield (Dickens)
   B: 66
Davis, Ross
   B: 32
Day parole
   A: 2: 320
De la Warr, Lord
   PS: 19–20
Death penalty. *See also* Capital
   punishment
   Bundy, Ted and, *B:* 37–38
   Darrow, Clarence and, *B:* 45,
     49
   Dickens, Charles and, *B:* 61,
     65
Death row. *See also* Capital pun-
   ishment; Executions
   A: 2: 313 (ill.), 313–14, 429
Debs, Eugene V.
   B: 48
Decentralized policing
   A: 2: 244
Declaration of Independence
   A: 1: 26 (ill.)
   PS: 14
"Dee." *See* Darrow, Clarence
Defendants
   Bill of Rights, *A: 2:* 232
   colonial period, *A: 1:* 12–13
   court-martials, *A: 2:* 331–32
   military justice, *A: 2:* 326
   right to a defense attorney, *A:*
     2: 299

Defense attorneys. *See also* Attorneys
   A: 1: 12; *2:* 298–99
Defense, criminal
   B: 143, 145
Defense to crime
   child abuse as, *A: 2:* 368
   intoxication as a, *PS:* 102
Definitions
   aggravated assault, *A: 1:* 68
   arson, *A: 1:* 88
   burglary, *A: 1:* 78
   forcible rape, *A: 1:* 70
   fraud, *A: 1:* 92, 94
   juveniles, *A: 2:* 343
   motor vehicle theft, *A: 1:* 85
   organized crime, *A: 1:* 113
   robbery, *A: 1:* 65–66
   stalking, *A: 1:* 71
   statutory rape, *A: 1:* 70
   terrorism, *A: 1:* 168
   white-collar crime, *A: 1:* 92
Delaware
   A: 1: 4–5
   PS: 116
Delayed notification search war-
   rants
   PS: 206
Democracy in America (de Toc-
   queville)
   B: 15
Democratic National Conven-
   tion
   A: 2: 257, 258 (ill.)
Democratic-Republicans
   PS: 54
Demonstration in support of the
   Scottsboro Boys
   PS: 162, 164 (ill.)
Demonstrations. *See* Protests
"Denial of service"
   A: 1: 195
Dentistry, forensic
   B: 122
Deoxyribonucleic acid (DNA)
   B: 120, 124 (ill.)
Department of Defense (DOD)
   PS: 194
Department of Justice (DOJ), *B:*
   90–91. *See also* Federal Bu-
   reau of Investigation (FBI)
   AMBER Alert, *PS:* 176, 177–79
   Antitrust Division, *PS:* 141

Arrestee Drug Abuse Monitoring (ADAM) Program, *A: 1:* 141–42

Bureau of Justice Statistics, *A: 2:* 413

Environmental and Natural Resources Division, Justice Department, *A: 1:* 158

Environmental Crimes Section, *A: 1:* 158

Office of Child Support Enforcement, *A: 2:* 374

terrorism, *A: 1:* 51–52

Department of State
PS: 201

DePauw University
B: 139

Dershowitz, Alan
A: 2: 449

Detectives. *See* Private investigators

Detention centers
A: 2: 349

Dewey decimal system
B: 91

Dewey, Thomas E.
B: **53–60,** 54 (ill.)

Diallo, Amadou
A: 2: 425

Dickens, Charles
A: 1: 31
B: **61–68,** 62 (ill.), 144
PS: 44, 57 (ill.), **57–64**

Dickens Fellowship
B: 61

Dickens, John
B: 62–63

Disability claims, fraudulent
A: 1: 102

Discipline, school
A: 2: 380

Discretionary powers of government
PS: 52

Discrimination, racial. *See* Race/ethnicity; specific groups

Dishonorable discharges
A: 2: 330

Disposition
A: 2: 304, 306

Distinguished Fellow of the American Academy of Forensic Science
B: 125

District attorneys. *See* Prosecutors

District courts
A: 2: 287, 289–90
B: 74

Diversity, religious
A: 2: 394–95

DNA (Deoxyribonucleic acid)
A: 2: 272–73, 273 (ill.), 276–77, 282
B: 120, 124 (ill.)

Documents, questioned
A: 2: 270, 276

DOJ (Department of Justice). *See* Department of Justice (DOJ)

Domestic communism
B: 92

Domestic terrorists, Kaczynski, Ted
B: 97–103

Domestic violence
A: 1: 69–70; *2:* 296–98

Domestic Violence Task Force
A: 2: 297

Dopamine
A: 1: 221

Double jeopardy
A: 1: 27
B: 174

Douglas, John
B: 123

Doyle, Arthur Conan
A: 2: 445

Draft riots of 1863, New York City
B: 184, 187–89, 190 (ill.)

Drexel Burnham Lambert
B: 19, 20–21, 22

Drinking and driving
PS: 101–2

Driving under the influence (DUI)
A: 1: 138–40

Drug Abuse Resistance Education (DARE)
A: 2: 262

Drug control
first efforts, *PS:* 88–89
Harrison Act, *PS:* 79

Drug courts
A: 2: 295–96

Drug Enforcement Administration (DEA)
A: 1: 145

Drug hearings
B: 110

Drug legalization
A: 1: 146–47

Drug trafficking, *PS:* 94, 96, 101, 147
global organized crime, *A: 1:* 128–29
marijuana seizure, *A: 1:* 115 (ill.)
motorcycle gangs, *A: 1:* 122
organized crime, *A: 1:* 114
seizure, *A: 1:* 142 (ill.)
by type of drug, *A: 1:* 142–46

Drug use
B: 178

Drugs and crime. *See also* "War on drugs"
A: 1: 78, 140–46, 224

Drummond, Edward
B: 143–44

Due process, *PS:* 49, 163
eighteenth century, *A: 1:* 19
Fifth Amendment, *A: 2:* 248
juveniles, *A: 2:* 294–95, 347

DUI (driving under the influence)
A: 1: 138–40

Durston, Charles
PS: 110–13

Dutch colonists
A: 1: 4

"Dutch Schultz." *See* Flegenheimer, Arthur

E

E. C. Knight Company
PS: 140

Earp, Wyatt
A: 1: 35

Earth First!
A: 1: 178

Earth Liberation Front (ELF)
A: 1: 178

EAS (Emergency Alert System)
PS: 176

East Coast street gangs
A: 1: 127–29

Eastern Cherokee Indians *vs.* U.S. government
B: 132

Ecodefense: A Field Guide to Monkeywrenching (Foreman)
A: 1: 177–78
Economic conditions and crime
PS: 71
Economic issues
crime rates and, A: 1: 63
crime theories, A: 1: 213–14
industrialization, A: 1: 28–29
New Deal, A: 1: 45
"Ecoterrorism"
A: 1: 177
Ecstasy
A: 1: 144–46
Edelman, Marian Wright
A: 2: 370, 370 (ill.)
Education
academic freedom, B: 49,
50–51
women and, B: 3, 135–36
Education and crime
A: 1: 214–15, 216 (ill.), 222
Eighteenth Amendment
A: 1: 117–18
**Eighteenth Amendment—
Prohibition of Intoxicat-
ing Liquors
PS: 98–102**
Eighth Amendment
A: 1: 28
PS: 103, 105
Eisenhower, Dwight
B: 59
Elderly
A: 2: 416
Electric chair
A: 2: 406
PS: 107 (ill.), 114 (ill.)
Electrocution
as cruel and unusual punish-
ment, PS: 106–7
development of, PS: 105
of Kemmler, William, PS:
108–15
process, PS: 107–8
Electronic automobile tracking
systems
A: 1: 87
Electronic commerce
A: 1: 193, 195–96
Electronic monitoring
A: 2: 318–19
Electronic surveillance. *See* Wire-
tapping

ELF (Earth Liberation Front)
A: 1: 178
Embezzlement
A: 1: 105
PS: 24
Emergency Alert System (EAS)
PS: 176
Emigrants
PS: 62 (ill.)
Employment and crime
A: 1: 222
Encryption
A: 1: 200
PS: 191, 193, 195–96, 199
Endangered Species Act
A: 1: 154
Enforcement. *See also* Policing
Magna Carta, PS: 11
Prohibition, PS: 100
Engineering Research Facility, FBI
A: 2: 279
England
charters, A: 1: 5
colonists from, A: 1: 3–4
control over colonists, A: 1:
23–25
criminal justice system, A: 1:
8–9
firearm identification, A: 2:
266–67
legal system, A: 1: 1, 27
police, A: 1: 34; 2: 246, 249
property crimes, A: 1: 75, 77
religion and criminal justice,
A: 2: 395
watchmen, A: 2: 247 (ill.)
English common law
A: 1: 9, 28; 2: 292, 395
English law
PS: 1–15
Enron
A: 1: 53, 107–8, 108 (ill.)
Entertainment industry
A: 1: 111
Environmental and Natural Resources Division, Justice Department
A: 1: 158–59
Environmental arson
A: 1: 89–90
Environmental crime
awareness of, A: 1: 148, 150
corporations, A: 1: 162–66
definition, A: 1: 151–52

laws regulating, A: 1: 152–57
Environmental Crime (Clifford)
A: 1: 152
Environmental enforcement
agencies
A: 1: 157–59
Environmental laws
A: 1: 150–51, 152–57, 160
Environmental Protection
Agency (EPA)
A: 1: 152, 156, 158 (ill.),
158–60, 161 (ill.)
Environmental terrorism
A: 1: 177–78
Epperson v. Arkansas
B: 51
Equal opportunities for women.
See Women's rights
Equal Suffrage Amendment
B: 132, 133, 137
Espionage
PS: 225–28
Espionage Act of 1917
A: 1: 42
B: 91
Esquire
B: 43
Estes v. Texas
A: 2: 443
Estimating the cost of crime
A: 2: 411–12
Ethanol concentration in alco-
holic beverages
A: 1: 139
Ethnicity. *See* Race/ethnicity
Europe, PS: 116
colonists from, A: 1: 3
punishment, A: 2: 392, 394
theft, A: 1: 77
European Union
PS: 116
Evans, Dan
B: 32
Evidence
court-martials, A: 2: 332
Evidence Response Team
Unit, FBI, A: 2: 277–78, 278
(ill.)
"exclusionary rule," A: 2: 260
gathering, A: 2: 281 (ill.)
trace, B: 122
Evolution
B: 48, 49, 50–51

"Examination of Sarah Good"
PS: 29–41
Excessive bail
A: 1: 28
PS: 49, 51
"Exclusionary rule"
A: 2: 259–60
B: 75
Excommunication
A: 1: 17–18
Executions. *See also* Capital punishment; Death penalty; Death row
methods of, *A: 2:* 406
race/ethnicity, *A: 2:* 427
rise in number of, *A: 2:* 403
witch-hunts, *A: 1:* 10
Exhibitionism
A: 1: 135
Explorers
A: 1: 1–2
Explosives. *See also* Bombs
A: 2: 273–74
Export rings, stolen car
A: 1: 86–87
Extortion
A: 1: 46
Exxon Valdez oil spill
A: 1: 149 (ill.), 150, 163–65, 164 (ill.)

F

Fair Labor Standards Act (FLSA)
A: 2: 362
Fair trial, right to
B: 166, 170, 174
Fair trials
A: 1: 27; *2:* 437, 439
Faith-based prisons
A: 2: 407
"Fallen angels"
B: 20
Family, *PS:* 127–28
crime and family relationships, *A: 1:* 218–19
parents, responsibilities of, *A: 2:* 359, 360
Family and Medical Leave Act
A: 2: 361, 370
Family courts
A: 2: 373

Family Planning Services and Population Act of 1970
PS: 84–85
"Far Worse Than Hanging"
PS: 106–17
Fatal Vision (McGinniss)
A: 2: 446
Faulkner, Abigail and Dorothy
PS: 40
FBI. *See* Federal Bureau of Investigation (FBI)
The FBI
B: 94
Fear of crime. *See also* Community crime prevention
juvenile violence, *A: 2:* 349
personal adjustments in behavior, *A: 1:* 55–56; *2:* 415–16
twenty-first century, *A: 2:* 407
women, *A: 2:* 232
Federal Bureau of Investigation (FBI)
AMBER Alert, *PS:* 178
anthrax investigation, *A: 1:* 183 (ill.)
antitrust and price-fixing cases, *A: 1:* 108–9
Chem-Bio Sciences Unit, *A: 2:* 276
CODIS Unit, *A: 2:* 276–77
Computer Analysis and Response Team, *A: 2:* 279
Computer Investigations and Threat Assessment Center, *PS:* 190, 194–95
computer use, *PS:* 199
Counterterrorism and Forensic Science Research Unit, *A: 2:* 277
crime laboratory, *A: 2:* 264, 268, 274, 282
criminal profiling, *B:* 123
cyber crime investigations, *PS:* 198–99
Cyber Investigations Unit, *A: 1:* 207
Darrow, Clarence and, *B:* 50
Engineering Research Facility, *A: 2:* 279
Evidence Response Team Unit, *A: 2:* 277–78, 278 (ill.)
expanded responsibilities, *A: 2:* 255

fingerprint database, *A: 2:* 277–78
Flegenheimer, Arthur and, *B:* 56
Hazardous Materials Response Unit, *A: 2:* 278
Hoover, J. Edgar and, *B:* 87–96, 92 (ill.)
Investigative and Prosecutive Graphics Unit, *A: 2:* 279, 282
Kaczynski, Ted and, *B:* 101, 102
Latent Prints Unit, *A: 2:* 274–76, 280–81
"most wanted" criminals, *B:* 94, 94 (ill.)
Organized Crime Section, *A: 1:* 129
paint unit, *A: 2:* 276
pathologist, *A: 2:* 265 (ill.)
Photographic Unit, *A: 2:* 277
Questioned Documents Unit, *A: 2:* 276, 282
responsibilities of, *A: 1:* 43–45
securities fraud, *A: 1:* 105
Structural Design Unit, *A: 2:* 279, 282
telemarketing fraud, *A: 1:* 102
Trace Evidence Unit, *A: 2:* 282
Truman, Harry S. and, *B:* 93
Federal capital crimes
A: 2: 403, 405
Federal Communications Commission
PS: 179
Federal courts
appeals courts, *A: 2:* 290
cameras, disallowance of, *A: 2:* 444
circuit courts, *A: 2:* 287
development of, *A: 2:* 284, 286
district courts, *A: 2:* 287
judges, *A: 2:* 286–87, 289
jurisdiction, *A: 2:* 288
role of, *A: 2:* 288
structure, *A: 2:* 288–89
system, *A: 1:* 25
Federal crimes. *See also* Criminal laws
Crimes Act of 1790, *A: 1:* 26–27

espionage, *A: 1:* 42

extortion, *A: 1:* 46

juveniles, *A: 2:* 340

kidnapping, *A: 1:* 45

motor vehicle theft, *A: 1:* 37, 42

robbing a national bank, *A: 1:* 45

sedition, *A: 1:* 42

selling of alcoholic beverages, *A: 1:* 38

taking stolen goods across state lines, *A: 1:* 46

tax fraud, *A: 1:* 42

transporting women across state lines, *A: 1:* 38, 42

Federal criminal justice system responsibilities, *A: 1:* 41

victim and witness protection, *A: 2:* 238–40

victims' compensation, *A: 2:* 235

victims' rights, *A: 2:* 238

Federal government

birth control information, distribution of, *PS:* 84–85

limitations on power of, *PS:* 42, 44, 51–53

Federal Industrial Institution for Women

A: 1: 42

Federal Insecticide, Fungicide, and Rodenticide Act

A: 1: 157

Federal law enforcement. *See also* Federal Bureau of Investigation (FBI); U.S. marshals

A: 1: 35, 35 (ill.), 41

Federal prisons

A: 1: 41, 42, 47; *2:* 308, 309

Federal Trade Commission (FTC)

A: 1: 196

PS: 141, 144

Federal Water Pollution Control Act Amendments

A: 1: 153–54

Federal Woman Suffrage Amendment of 1878

B: 137

The Federalist Papers

PS: 47

Felonies

A: 1: 9; *2:* 330–31

Felony-murder rule

A: 1: 62

Fences

A: 1: 79

Ferris, Nathan

A: 2: 381

Feudal society

PS: 6

Fiction

A: 2: 444–46

Fifth Amendment

A: 1: 27; *2:* 248, 260

B: 104, 147, 151

Films. *See* Movies

Films, gangster

PS: 151

Finances and counterterrorism

PS: 204–5, 208, 210

Financial Action Task Force

PS: 205

Financial institution fraud

A: 1: 97–100

Financiers

B: 17–23

Financing of terrorism

A: 1: 172, 187

Fines

PS: 10

Fingerprints

A: 2: 245 (ill.), 266, 269, 275 (ill.), 280–81

Fire setting. *See also* Arson

A: 1: 178

Firearms, *A: 1:* 199, 224, 225 (ill.); *2:* 387, 388–89; *B:* 113, 114–15, 116. *See also* Weapons

Gun Control Act, *A: 1:* 199

gun sales, *A: 1:* 199

identification, *A: 2:* 266–67, 268, 269 (ill.), 280

First Amendment

A: 1: 135

B: 51

Fishermen

PS: 25

Flamingo (casino)

A: 1: 117

Flegenheimer, Arthur

B: 55, 56–57, 57 (ill.)

Fleiss, Heidi

B: 182, 182 (ill.)

Fleiss, Paul

B: 182

Flexible sentencing

A: 2: 404

FLSA (Fair Labor Standards Act)

A: 2: 362

Folk Nation

A: 1: 127

Food, Drug, and Cosmetic Act

A: 1: 198

Forcible entry

A: 1: 78, 79 (ill.)

Forcible rape

A: 1: 70–71

Foreclosure scams

A: 1: 103

Foreign Terrorist Asset Tracking Center

PS: 205

Foreign Terrorist Organizations

A: 1: 188–89

PS: 204, 231

Foreman, Dave

A: 1: 177–78

Forensic dentistry

A: 2: 271–72

B: 122

Forensic medicine

B: 122

Forensic science. *See also* Crime laboratories

B: 120–26

Forensic toxicology

B: 122

Forensic voiceprinting

B: 122

Forfeiture of property

drug crimes, *PS:* 95

Racketeer Influenced and Corrupt Organizations (RICO) Act, *PS:* 151

Sherman Antitrust Act, *PS:* 139

Forgery

A: 1: 99

Fort Peck Reservation

A: 2: 336

Foster care

A: 2: 369

Fourteenth Amendment

A: 1: 36

Fourth Amendment

A: 1: 27; *2:* 248

France, *B:* 10, 11–12

British defeat of, *A: 1:* 23, 25

crime laboratory, *A: 2:* 267

police, *A: 2:* 246

Frankfurter, Emma

B: 70, 71

Frankfurter, Felix

B: 69–77, 70 (ill.)

Franks, Bobby

B: 49

PS: 118, 120, 124

Fraud

bankruptcy, *A: 1:* 103

credit card, *A: 1:* 196–97

credit card loss protection

scams, *A: 1:* 101

disability claims, *A: 1:* 102

financial institution, *A: 1:*
97–100

government, *A: 1:* 96–97

healthcare, *A: 1:* 94–96

insurance, *A: 1:* 102–3

Internet, *A: 1:* 195–97

loan, *A: 1:* 98–100

online auction, *A: 1:* 196 (ill.)

securities, *A: 1:* 106–7, 201–2

tax, *A: 1:* 42

telemarketing, *A: 1:* 102

Free market economies

PS: 134

Free speech

B: 8, 83, 110

Free Speech League

B: 83

Freedom of the press

B: 170

PS: 49

Freeh, Louis J.

A: 2: 431 (ill.)

PS: 188–89, **190–97,** 193 (ill.)

French and Indian War

A: 1: 23

French Revolution

B: 10, 11

Frick, Henry Clay

B: 81–82

Frontier life

A: 1: 6–8

FTC (Federal Trade Commission)

PS: 141, 144

The Fugitive

B: 170, 175

Fuhrman, Mark

A: 2: 449

Full Faith and Credit for Child
Support Orders Act
A: 2: 370, 374

Fuller, Melville
PS: 107

Funding

AMBER Alert, **PS:** 180–81

counterterrorism, *A: 2:* 417

terrorist, **PS:** 205, 208

Tribal Courts Program, *A: 2:*
338

Furlough
A: 2: 320

Furman v. Georgia
A: 2: 404

Future of juvenile justice
A: 2: 355–56

G

Gadge, Sarah and Thomas
PS: 35–36, 38–39

Gambino crime family
A: 1: 121
PS: 153 (ill.)

Gambling
A: 1: 199–200
B: 178
PS: 78

Gang rape
A: 1: 72

Gangs. *See also* Street gangs
PS: 100

Gangster Disciples
A: 1: 127–28

Gangsters. *See also* Organized
crime; Street gangs
PS: 150–51

Gardner, Erle Stanley
A: 2: 445–46, 446 (ill.)

Gates, Bill
PS: 143 (ill.)

Gates, Sir Thomas
PS: 20

G-8 nations
PS: 205

Gender and murder
A: 1: 64

General court-martials
A: 2: 330–31

General Crimes Act
A: 2: 334–35

General Intelligence Division
(GID)
B: 90–91

General Motors Corporation
A: 1: 163

Genetics and crime
A: 1: 219–20

Genocide
A: 1: 173

Genocide Convention
A: 2: 297

Geoghan, John
A: 2: 371

Georgia
A: 2: 405

"Get tough" policies

capital punishment, *A: 2:* 405

growing prison population, *A:
2:* 310–11

juvenile justice, *A: 2:* 347–49

megaprisons, *A: 2:* 311–12

police, public attitudes regard-
ing, *A: 2:* 260–61

repeat offenders, *A: 1:* 73

Gilley, Orville
PS: 167, 168

Giuliani, Rudolph "Rudy"
B: 22

Global Positioning Systems
(GPS)
A: 1: 206 (ill.); *2:* 319

"G-Men"
B: 93

Goddard, Henry
A: 2: 266–67

The Godfather (film)
A: 1: 111, 112 (ill.); *2:* 446

Golden, Andrew
A: 2: 383

Goldman, Emma
B: 78–86, 79 (ill.), 81 (ill.)

Goldman, Ronald
A: 2: 448, 449

Good, Sarah
PS: 34–39

Gotti, John
A: 1: 121
PS: 154

Gotti, Peter
A: 1: 121

Government claims
A: 2: 412

Government fraud
A: 1: 96–97

Governor, Dewey, Thomas E. as
B: 53, 56, 59
GPS (Global Positioning Systems)
A: 1: 206 (ill.); *2:* 319
Grand juries
A: 1: 9, 27; *2:* 300–1
Grand larceny
A: 1: 81
Grant, Ulysses
B: 129–30
Grants for AMBER Alert programs
PS: 179–81
Gravano, Salvatore
A: 1: 121, 121 (ill.)
PS: 154
Gray, Abby Durfee
B: 24–26, 29
"Great Charter"
PS: 26
Great Depression, *B:* 180–81
murder rates, *A: 1:* 63
prisons, *A: 1:* 48–49
Great European Witch-hunt
PS: 29
Great Expectations (Dickens)
B: 66
Greece, ancient
A: 1: 131, 133
Green, Joseph
PS: 40
Green Light Gangs
A: 1: 127
Gregg v. Georgia
A: 2: 405
Guilty pleas
PS: 124
Guns. *See* Firearms

H

Hackers
A: 1: 194
PS: 189 (ill.), 192–93
Hagen, Chris M. *See* Bundy, Ted
Hagerman, Amber
PS: 173, 174
Halfway houses
A: 2: 319 (ill.), 320
HAMAS
A: 1: 170, 181–82

Hamilton, Alexander
A: 2: 439
PS: 47
Handguns. *See* Firearms
Hanging, *A: 1:* 16, 29; *2:* 406;
PS: 104 (ill.)
as cruel and unusual punishment, *PS:* 103, 105
electrocution *vs., PS:* 114
society, effect on, *PS:* 125–26
Harding, Tonya
A: 2: 317 (ill.)
Hare, Robert
A: 1: 220
Harlan, John Marshall
A: 2: 443
Harm, environmental
A: 1: 151–52
Harriman, E. H.
PS: 141
Harris, Eric
A: 2: 379 (ill.), 385
B: 114
Harrison Narcotic Drug Act of 1914
PS: **88–97**
Hate crimes
A: 1: 62; *2:* 433–35
Hathorne, John
PS: 35
Hauptmann, Bruno Richard
A: 1: 45; *2:* 441–42
Hawkins, Georgann
B: 35
Hayes, Rutherford
B: 130
Haymarket trials
B: 81
Haywood, William Dudley
B: 49, 83, 84–85, 85 (ill.)
Hazardous Materials Response Unit, FBI
A: 2: 278
Hazardous waste
A: 1: 154–57, 155 (ill.), 158 (ill.), 159, 160–61
Head Start
A: 2: 361
Healthcare
A: 2: 362
Healthcare fraud
A: 1: 94–96
Healy, Lynda Ann
B: 35

Hearst, William Randolph
A: 2: 440
Hell's Angels
A: 1: 122–23, 123 (ill.)
Henry C. Lee Institute of Forensic Science
B: 120, 125
Hepburn, Audrey
B: 41
Herbal ecstasy pills
A: 1: 146 (ill.)
Heredity and crime
A: 1: 219–20
Heresy
A: 1: 15
Heroin
A: 1: 143
PS: 90, 93
Hezbollah
A: 1: 170
Hickcock, Richard, tombstone
B: 44 (ill.)
Hiding places, terrorist
PS: 220–21
High school drug abuse trends
A: 1: 141
Hijacking
A: 1: 184
PS: 198
Hill, James J.
PS: 141
Hinckley, John
B: 143
Hispanic Americans
A: 1: 126–27, 127 (ill.); *2:* 422, 429
Hogarth, William, engraving by
B: 144 (ill.)
"Hollywood Madam"
B: 182, 182 (ill.)
Holmes, Sherlock (character)
A: 2: 445
Home care agencies
A: 1: 94–95
Home security systems
A: 1: 218 (ill.)
Homeland Security Advisory System
A: 1: 185 (ill.)
Homeland Security, Department of
A: 1: 51, 185; *2:* 417
PS: 186, 211
Homicide. *See* Murder

Homicide/murder distinction
  A: 1: 61–62
Honeymoon Gang
  B: 185
Hooker Chemical Company
  A: 1: 150
Hookers. See Streetwalkers
Hoon, Geoff
  PS: 227
Hoover, Herbert
  A: 1: 39, 43; 2: 254, 411
  PS: 66–67, 70
Hoover, J. Edgar
  A: 1: 42, 43–44, 44 (ill.),
    119–20; 2: 255, 269
  B: 83–84, **87–96**, 88 (ill.), 92
    (ill.)
Hormones
  A: 1: 221–22
Horton, James
  B: 166, 168
  PS: 163, 167
Hostages
  A: 1: 180
  PS: 226
House arrest
  A: 2: 318
House of Burgesses
  A: 1: 4
  PS: 27
House of Flowers (Capote)
  B: 41
House Un-American Activities
    Committee (HUAC)
  B: 95
Household appliances, dumping
    of
  A: 1: 162
Household Words
  B: 66
Hsi Yüan Lu (book)
  A: 2: 266
Hubbard, Elizabeth
  PS: 35, 36
Hull House
  B: 5, 6 (ill.), 8
Hung juries
  A: 2: 302
Hunt, Ward
  B: 137
Hussein, Saddam
  PS: 211
Hutson, Melvin C.
  PS: 164, 165, 166, 168

I

IAFIS (Integrated Automated
    Fingerprint Identification
    System)
  A: 2: 275–76, 281
IC3 (Internet Crime Complain
    Center)
  A: 1: 207–8
Identity and cyber crime
  A: 1: 207–8
Identity theft
  A: 1: 196 (ill.), 196–97
Ideology
  PS: 218
ILD (International Labor De-
    fense)
  B: 165, 166
Illegal search and seizure
  B: 75
Illinois
  A: 2: 294, 343
Illinois Central Railroad
  B: 157
Illinois juvenile justice system
  B: 1, 5
ImClone Systems Inc.
  A: 1: 106
Immigrants
  A: 2: 419, 421
Impersonation
  A: 1: 98–99
Imports and exports
  PS: 92
In Cold Blood (Capote)
  A: 2: 446
  B: 39, 41–42, 43
Incarceration
  A: 2: 308–11
Indian Country
  A: 2: 334–38
Indian Reorganization Act
  A: 2: 335
Indians. See Native Americans
Individual terrorism
  A: 1: 178–79
Individuals with Disabilities Ed-
    ucation Act
  A: 2: 362
Industrial civilization
  B: 97
"Industrial Society and Its Fu-
    ture" (Kaczynski)
  B: 97, 103

Industrial Workers of the World
    (IWW)
  B: 84, 85
Industrialization
  A: 1: 28–29
Information gathering
  on Al Qaeda, PS: 204
  by terrorists, PS: 225–28
Information sharing
  counterterrorism, PS: 205, 207
  law enforcement agencies, PS:
    207
Infrastructure protection
  PS: 184, 186, 189, 194
Inherit the Wind
  B: 51
Inheritance
  PS: 10
Inner-city schools
  A: 2: 380–81
Innocent Images case
  PS: 193
Innocent III, Pope
  PS: 7
Insanity defense
  B: 143, 145
Insider trading
  A: 1: 105–6
  B: 17, 19, 20–22
Insurance
  arson, A: 1: 89
  claims, A: 2: 412
  fraud, A: 1: 102–3
Intangible costs of crime
  A: 2: 409
Integrated Automated Finger-
    print Identification System
    (IAFIS)
  A: 2: 275–76, 281
Intellectual property
  A: 1: 54–55, 202–5
  PS: 195
Intelligence gathering
  A: 1: 186
Intensive Probation Supervision
    (IPS)
  A: 2: 317–18
Intent to defraud
  A: 1: 88
Interior, Department of the
  A: 2: 334
Internal insurance fraud
  A: 1: 102–3

International Computer Crime
   Conference
   PS: 188
International copyright agree-
   ments
   B: 63–64
International courts
   A: 2: 297
International crime organizations
   PS: 154
International issues
   capital punishment, *PS:* 116
   child abduction, *A: 2:* 365–66
   counterterrorism, *PS:* 203–5,
      208–10, 211, 212
   cyber crime, *A: 1:* 206–7
   intellectual property theft, *A:
      1:* 205
   law enforcement, *PS:* 197
   Legal Attaché program, *PS:*
      196
   motorcycle gangs, *A: 1:*
      122–23
   organized crime, *A: 1:* 113,
      128–29
   terrorism, *A: 1:* 168, 170
   terrorism sponsors, *PS:* 210
   "War on Terror," *PS:* 186, 190
International Labor Defense
   (ILD)
   B: 165, 166
   PS: 162–63
International organized crime
   B: 109
International Peace Congresses
   B: 132
International Policewoman's As-
   sociation
   A: 1: 37
International Revenue Service
   (IRS)
   A: 2: 254
Internet
   abduction, child, *PS:* 193
   anti-pornography laws, *PS:* 86
   child pornography, *A: 1:*
      197–98
   crime and access to informa-
      tion, *A: 1:* 224–25
   crimes, *PS:* 189
   cyber crime, *A: 1:* 54–55
   encryption, *A: 1:* 200
   fraud, *A: 1:* 195–97

Internet service providers
   (ISPs), *A: 1:* 197
   overview, *A: 1:* 191, 193
   pornography, *A: 1:* 136
   protection of children, *A: 2:*
      376
   securities fraud, *A: 1:* 106–7
Internet Crime Complain Cen-
   ter (IC3)
   A: 1: 207–8
Interstate crime
   A: 1: 45–46
Intolerance
   B: 7
Intoxication as a defense to
   crime
   PS: 102
Investigations and computer
   technology
   PS: 192
Investigations
   cyber crime, *A: 1:* 193
   MDMA trafficking, *A: 1:*
      145–46
Investigative and Prosecutive
   Graphics Unit, FBI
   A: 2: 279, 282
Involuntary manslaughter
   A: 1: 63
Iowa, law licenses in
   B: 138–39
Iowa Women's Hall of Fame
   B: 134
IPS (Intensive Probation Supervi-
   sion)
   A: 2: 317–18
Iran
   A: 1: 180
Iraq, war in
   PS: 211
IRS (International Revenue Ser-
   vice)
   A: 2: 254
Islam
   PS: 216–17, 218, 226
Islamic religious terrorism
   A: 1: 171–72
Isolation, prison
   PS: 58–63
ISPs (Internet service providers)
   A: 1: 197
Israel
   A: 1: 182–83

Ivan F. Boesky Corporation
   B: 19
IWW (Industrial Workers of the
   World)
   B: 84, 85

J

J. Edgar Hoover Building
   B: 88, 95
Jackson, Andrew
   B: 14
Jackson, Michael
   A: 2: 447
Jackson, Thomas Penfield
   PS: 142
Jails
   A: 1: 18, 31; *2:* 308–9, 338
James I
   PS: 13, 17
Jamestown, Virginia
   A: 1: 6–8, 7 (ill.)
   PS: 18–20, 26–27
Japan
   PS: 116
Japanese Americans
   A: 2: 431
Jay, John
   PS: 47
Jefferson, Thomas
   A: 1: 26 (ill.)
   PS: 54
Jenkins, W. T.
   PS: 114–15
Jihad
   PS: 217
Jim Crow laws
   A: 2: 422
Job training
   A: 1: 215
John, King of England
   PS: 1, 2 (ill.), 5–8, 8 (ill.), 12–13
Johnson, Abigail and Stephen
   PS: 40
Johnson, Lyndon B.
   A: 1: 53, 80; *2:* 257
   PS: 133
Johnson, Mitchell
   A: 2: 383
Journey to the Far Pacific (Dewey)
   B: 59
Judge Advocate General (JAG)
   A: 2: 326, 332, 333, 334

Judges
    cameras in the courtroom, *A: 2:* 444, 450
    colonial period, *A: 1:* 11–12
    federal courts, *A: 2:* 289
    juvenile courts, *A: 2:* 349
    military, *A: 2:* 332–33
    state courts, *A: 2:* 292–94
Judicial restraint
    B: 76–77
Judiciary Act of 1789
    A: 1: 26; *2:* 287
    B: 74
"The Junk Bond King." *See* Milken, Michael
Junk bonds
    B: 20, 21
Juries, *PS:* 163, 164, 166, 169. *See also* Trial by jury
    colonial period, *A: 1:* 12
    eighteenth century, *A: 1:* 19
Jurisdiction
    cyber crime, *A: 1:* 205–7
    federal courts, *A: 2:* 288
    juvenile courts, *A: 2:* 294, 340, 342
    military justice, *A: 2:* 328
    Native Americans, *A: 2:* 334–35, 336
    Racketeer Influenced and Corrupt Organizations (RICO) Act, *PS:* 151
    Sherman Antitrust Act, *PS:* 139–40
    state courts, *A: 2:* 287
Jury awards
    A: 2: 411–12
Jury tampering
    B: 48–49
Jury trials
    A: 1: 12; *2:* 295
Justices of the peace. *See* Magistrates
Justifiable homicide
    A: 1: 62
Justification defense
    B: 143
Juvenile Court Act (Illinois)
    A: 1: 56
Juvenile courts, *PS:* 71–72
    case transfers to adult courts, *A: 2:* 295, 345, 353–54, 354 (ill.)
    civil liberties, *A: 2:* 346–47

establishment of, *A: 2:* 294–95
    judges, *A: 2:* 349
    jurisdiction, *A: 2:* 340, 342
    overview, *A: 2:* 343–46
    proceedings, *A: 2:* 349–51
    rights of juveniles, *A: 2:* 349–51, 375–76
    sentencing, *A: 2:* 351–52
Juvenile Courts Act
    A: 2: 345
Juvenile crime
    arson, *A: 1:* 88–89
    causes, *A: 2:* 355
    delinquents, *A: 2:* 341 (ill.)
    Juvenile Delinquency Prevention Act, *A: 1:* 56; *2:* 347
    rates of, *A: 2:* 356
    statistics, *A: 2:* 344–45
Juvenile justice system, *B:* 1, 5
    future of, *A: 2:* 355–56
    get-tough policies, *A: 1:* 57
    Juvenile Court Act (Illinois), *A: 1:* 56
    juvenile prisons, *A: 2:* 348 (ill.)

K

Kaashmir
    A: 1: 184
Kaczynski, David
    B: 100, 103
Kaczynski, Ted
    A: 1: 51, 179, 179 (ill.); *2:* 279
    B: **97–103**, 98 (ill.),101 (ill.)
Kanka, Megan
    A: 2: 365
    PS: 182
Kansas City Massacre
    PS: 191
Kashmir
    A: 1: 170–71
Kefauver Committee
    A: 1: 50 (ill.), 120
    B: 104–5, 107–9, 107 (ill.)
Kefauver, Estes
    A: 1: 49
    B: **104–10**, 105 (ill.), 107 (ill.)
Kefauver-Harris Drug Control Act of 1962
    B: 110

Kemmler, William
    A: 2: 406
    PS: 106–16
Kempe, Henry
    A: 2: 367
Kennedy, John A.
    B: 188
Kennedy, Robert
    A: 1: 50, 120
Kent, Debbie
    B: 35
Kent v. U.S.
    A: 2: 353
Kersner, Jacob
    B: 80
Khobar Towers bombing
    A: 1: 181
Kidnapping. *See also* Abduction; Lindbergh baby kidnapping
    A: 1: 179–80; *2:* 363–66
    B: 35, 36, 149–50, 152–53
Kilby Prison
    PS: 171
Kill switches
    A: 1: 87
Killers. *See* Murder; Serial killers
Killing of hostages
    PS: 226
King, Martin Luther, Jr.
    A: 2: 424
    B: 95
King, Rodney
    A: 1: 55; *2:* 424–25
King's authority
    PS: 8, 17–18
Kinkel, Bill
    B: 111, 113, 114, 116
Kinkel, Faith
    B: 111, 113, 116–17
Kinkel, Kip
    A: 1: 61, 65; *2:* 383–84, 384 (ill.)
    B: **111–19**, 112 (ill.), 117 (ill.)
Klebold, Dylan
    A: 2: 379 (ill.), 385
    B: 114
Knight, Thomas E., Jr.
    PS: 164
Knox, Philander C.
    PS: 140
Kollar-Kotelly, Colleen
    PS: 142
Kroeger, Brooke
    B: 82

Ku Klux Klan
    A: 1: 176; 2: 434 (ill.)

L

La Cosa Nostra
    PS: 133, 191
La Guardia, Fiorello
    B: 55
L. A. Law (TV show)
    A: 2: 447
Labeling of medicines
    PS: 89
Labor disputes. See also Organized labor
    B: 160, 190
Labor movement. See Organized labor
Labor racketeering
    A: 1: 119–20
The Lady of the House (Stanford)
    B: 183
Lafayette, Marquis de
    B: 15
Lakeview NeuroRehabilitation Center
    A: 2: 319 (ill.)
Land barons
    PS: 1, 5–8, 12–13
Langton, Stephen
    PS: 7
Lansky, Meyer
    A: 1: 117, 119
Larceny-theft
    A: 1: 77, 81–85
Las Vegas, Nevada
    A: 1: 117
Latent prints
    A: 2: 269
Latent Prints Unit, FBI
    A: 2: 274–76, 280–81
Latin Kings
    A: 1: 127
Law & Order (TV show)
    A: 2: 447
Law, Bernard
    A: 2: 371, 372, 372 (ill.)
Law enforcement. See also Policing
    computer technology, use of, PS: 189
    cooperation between agencies, PS: 198

corruption, PS: 73, 74, 75
counterterrorism, PS: 204
evidence-sharing, PS: 207
jurisdictions, PS: 186
terrorism prevention, PS: 184–85
USA Patriot Act, PS: 206
Wickersham Commission, PS: 44–45
Law Enforcement Assistance Administration (LEAA)
    A: 1: 53; 2: 258
"Lawes Divine, Morall and Martiall"
    A: 1: 7–8
    PS: 17–28
Laws and Liberties of Massachusetts
    A: 1: 14
Laws, discriminatory
    PS: 171
Lawsuits. See also Settlements, lawsuit
    antitrust, PS: 142
    children, A: 2: 375–76
    estimating cost of crime by, A: 2: 411–12
    Racketeer Influenced and Corrupt Organizations (RICO) Act, PS: 152
    Sherman Antitrust Act, PS: 139
    victims, A: 2: 233
Lawtey Correctional Institution
    A: 2: 399 (ill.)
Lawyers. See Attorneys
LEAA (Law Enforcement Assistance Administration)
    A: 1: 53; 2: 258
Leach, Kimberly Diane
    B: 35, 36, 37
Leavenworth Federal Penitentiary
    A: 2: 308
Lee, Henry C.
    B: 120–26, 121 (ill.), 124 (ill.)
Legal Attaché offices
    A: 1: 186
Legal Attaché program
    PS: 196
Legal dramas
    A: 2: 447, 450
Legal system, juvenile
    B: 1, 5
Legalization of drugs
    A: 1: 146–47

"Legat" offices
    A: 1: 186
"Legat" program
    PS: 196
Lehman, Herbert H.
    B: 57
Leibowitz, Samuel
    B: 165, 165 (ill.), 166, 168
    PS: 161 (ill.), 163, 164, 167
Lenin, Vladimir
    B: 84
Leopold, Nathan
    B: 49
    PS: 118, 119 (ill.), 120–29, 121 (ill.)
Lethal injection
    A: 2: 406
    PS: 116
Levine, Dennis
    B: 19, 22
Levy, Lisa
    B: 35, 37, 37 (ill.)
LGT Bank
    A: 1: 129 (ill.)
License suspension
    A: 1: 140
Life imprisonment
    PS: 128–29
Life Plus 99 Years (Leopold)
    PS: 129
Lifetime Achievement Award
    B: 125
Lightner, Candace
    A: 2: 230 (ill.)
Lincoln, Abraham
    A: 2: 280
    B: 157, 157 (ill.)
Lindbergh Act
    A: 1: 45
Lindbergh baby kidnapping
    A: 1: 45; 2: 364, 364 (ill.), 403, 440–42, 441 (ill.)
Lindh, John Walker
    PS: 204
Literacy
    A: 1: 19
Literary nonfiction
    B: 39, 42–43
Little Caesar (film)
    PS: 151
Living My Life (Goldman)
    B: 85
Lizzie Borden Bed and Breakfast
    B: 27 (ill.)

Loan fraud
  A: 1: 98–100
Lobotomy
  A: 1: 219 (ill.)
Local law enforcement
  PS: 179
Locard, Edmund
  A: 2: 267
Locking mechanisms
  A: 1: 87, 87 (ill.)
Lockwood, Belva Ann
  B: 127–33, 128 (ill.)
Lockwood, Ezekiel
  B: 129
Loeb, Richard
  B: 49
  PS: 118, 119 (ill.), 120–29,
  121 (ill.)
Lombroso, Cesare
  A: 1: 212
London's Bethlem Hospital
  B: 144 (ill.), 145
Los Angeles, California
  Hispanic gangs, A: 1: 126–27
  police, A: 2: 267, 423 (ill.),
  424–25
  Rodney King riots, A: 1: 55
  street gangs, A: 1: 123–26
  women police, A: 1: 35, 37
"Lost Colony"
  A: 1: 3
Louis Phillipe, King of France
  B: 10, 11, 12
Louisiana
  A: 2: 292
Louisiana state penitentiary
  A: 1: 46 (ill.)
Loukaitis, Barry
  A: 2: 381–82
Love Canal
  A: 1: 150
Lower courts
  A: 2: 292
Lucchese crime family
  PS: 148 (ill.)
Luciano, Charles "Lucky"
  A: 1: 119, 120 (ill.)
  B: 55

M

MacDonald, Carlos F.
  PS: 112

MacLaren Youth Correctional
  Facility
  B: 118
MacNaughten, Daniel. See Mc-
  Naughtan, Daniel
Madam Alex
  B: 182
Madams
  A: 1: 134
  B: 177, 180–81, 182, 183
MADD (Mothers Against Drunk
  Driving)
  A: 2: 236
Madison, James, PS: 47 (ill.)
  "Amendments to the Consti-
  tution," PS: 48–53
  Articles of Confederation, PS:
  46–47
Mafia. See American Mafia; Or-
  ganized crime
Magistrates
  A: 1: 11–12; 2: 286, 289–90
Magna Carta
  A: 1: 14
  PS: 5–16, 12 (ill.)
Mai Phuong Lee
  A: 1: 145
"Mailbombing"
  A: 1: 195
Major Crimes Act
  A: 2: 334
Malvo, Lee Boyd
  A: 2: 280–82
Mandatory sentencing
  A: 1: 54; 2: 310–11
  PS: 95
Mann Act of 1910
  A: 1: 37, 42
  B: 179
  PS: 86
Mann Act of 1986
  B: 179
Mansfield, Arabella
  B: 134–40
Mansfield, John Melvin
  B: 135, 138, 139
Manslaughter/murder distinction
  A: 1: 62–63
Manson, Donna Gail
  B: 35
Marie (de Beaumont)
  B: 15
Marijuana
  A: 1: 143

PS: 95
Marine Protection Research and
  Sanctuaries Act
  A: 1: 154
Marital rape
  A: 1: 72
Market manipulation, securities
  A: 1: 201
Marriage, common-law
  B: 153
Marshall, John
  A: 2: 439
The Marshalsea
  B: 62–63
Maryland
  A: 1: 4
The Mask of Sanity (Cleckley)
  A: 1: 213
Mason, Perry (character)
  A: 2: 445–46
Mass murder
  A: 1: 65
Massachusetts, PS: 142–43
  state police, A: 2: 256
  state prison, A: 1: 30–31
Material support of terrorism
  PS: 207
Mattison, Jack
  B: 118
Maximum security prisons
  A: 2: 312–13
Mayflower Compact
  A: 1: 2 (ill.), 4
McComb, Charles
  PS: 161 (ill.)
McGinniss, Joe
  A: 2: 446
McKenna, James
  B: 159
McKinley, William
  B: 82–83
McNall's Academy
  B: 129
McNaughtan, Daniel
  B: 141–46
McNaughtan Rules
  B: 141, 143, 145
McNaughton, Daniel. See Mc-
  Naughtan, Daniel
McNaughtun, Daniel. See Mc-
  Naughtan, Daniel
McParland, James
  B: 159

McVeigh, Timothy
   A: 1: 51, 176, 178, 181
MDMA
   A: 1: 144–46
Media
   Arbuckle trial, *A: 2:* 439–40
   books, television and movies,
     A: 2: 444–47
   Borden, Lizzie and, *B:* 28,
     29–30
   Burr trial, *A: 2:* 439
   cameras in the courtroom, *A:*
     2: 442–44, 448–49
   fair trials and, *A: 2:* 437, 439
   Kefauver Committee and, *B:*
     108–9
   Lindbergh baby kidnapping,
     A: 2: 440–42, 441 (ill.)
   murder trial coverage, *A: 2:*
     447–49
   school violence, *B:* 114–15
   Scopes trial, *B:* 50–51
   Sheppard, Sam and, *B:* 170,
     173–75
   true crime, *B:* 42–43
Mediation
   A: 2: 237
Medicaid program
   A: 2: 362
Medical issues
   A: 1: 150
Medicare health fraud
   A: 1: 94–96
Medici, Catherine de
   A: 2: 267
Medicine, forensic
   B: 122
Megan's Law
   A: 2: 365
   PS: 182
Megaprisons
   A: 2: 311–12
Meghan's Law. *See* Megan's Law
Memorial service
   A: 1: 60 (ill.)
Menendez, Erik and Lyle
   A: 2: 368
Mental capacity
   PS: 72
"Merchant privilege law"
   A: 1: 83
Merrill Lynch
   A: 1: 106

Merton, Robert K.
   A: 1: 214–15
Metal detectors
   A: 2: 390 (ill.)
Metallurgy units
   A: 2: 270
Methamphetamines
   A: 1: 143–44, 144 (ill.)
Mexican Mafia
   A: 1: 127
Michel Prison
   A: 2: 394
Michigan
   abolition of capital punish-
     ment, *A: 2:* 402
   death penalty, abolition of
     the, *A: 1:* 31
Michigan v. Lucas
   A: 1: 72
Micro-Cap
   A: 1: 106
Microsoft Corporation
   PS: 142–43
Middle Ages
   A: 2: 392, 393, 394
Middle Eastern countries
   PS: 116
Middle school drug abuse trends
   A: 1: 141
Midwest street gangs
   A: 1: 127–29
Military coalition. *See* Coalition
   forces
Military justice, *A: 2:* 323 (ill.)
   appeals, *A: 2:* 325, 333–34
   Articles of War, *A: 2:* 324
   Constitution, U.S., *A: 2:*
     324–25
   court-martials, *A: 2:* 326,
     329–33, 330 (ill.)
   development of, *A: 2:* 322, 324
   Uniform Code of Military Jus-
     tice (UCMJ), *A: 2:* 328
   Wirz, Henry, trial of, *A: 2:*
     325 (ill.)
Military Justice Act
   A: 2: 333
Military organization, Al
   Qaeda's
   PS: 217–18
Military police
   A: 2: 325 (ill.), 327, 332 (ill.)
Militia movement
   A: 1: 175–76

Milken, Michael
   B: 19, 20–21, 21 (ill.), 22, 23
Miller, B. M.
   B: 164
Miranda, Ernest
   B: **147–53**, 148 (ill.)
Miranda Rights
   A: 2: 259–60
   B: 75, 147, 150–52, 152 (ill.)
Miranda v. Arizona
   B: 147, 150, 151
Miranda Warning. *See* Miranda
   Rights
Mirror of Parliament
   B: 63
Misdemeanors
   A: 1: 9, 134
Mission of Al Qaeda
   PS: 218
Mistrial, motion for
   PS: 166
Mitnik, Kevin
   PS: 192
M'Naghten, Daniel. *See* Mc-
   Naughtan, Daniel
Mob. *See* American Mafia
The Molly Maguires
   B: 158–59, 160
Money laundering
   A: 1: 114–15
   PS: 147, 205
Money Laundering Control Act
   of 1986
   B: 109
The Monkey Wrench Gang (Abbey)
   A: 1: 177–78
Monopolies, *B:* 110
   American Telephone and
     Telegraph (AT&T), *PS:* 143
   Microsoft, *PS:* 142–43
   Sherman Antitrust Act, *PS:*
     134, 138, 145
   Standard Oil of New Jersey v.
     United States, PS: 135
Montana
   A: 1: 166–67
   B: 99–101
Montgomery, Olen
   B: 162, 169
   PS: 160, 168, 170, 170 (ill.)
Monthly Magazine
   B: 63
Moody, William H.
   B: 28, 28 (ill.), 29

Moody's
  B: 20
Moore, Michael
  A: 2: 385
Moral offenses. See also Public
    order crimes
  Comstock law, PS: 80–87
  Harrison Act, PS: 88–97
  overview, PS: 76–79
  Prohibition, PS: 98–102
Morality
  capital punishment, A: 2: 401
  ethics, standards of, A: 2: 394
Morgan, J. P.
  PS: 141
Morrow, Anne
  A: 2: 440
Mother Earth
  B: 83
Mothers Against Drunk Driving
    (MADD)
  A: 1: 138; 2: 236
Mothers as primary caregivers
  A: 2: 361
Motives
  robbery, A: 1: 66
  theft, A: 1: 78–79
  white-collar crime, A: 1: 92
Motor vehicle accessories, theft of
  A: 1: 82
Motor vehicle theft
  A: 1: 38, 42, 75, 77, 85 (ill.),
    85–88, 87 (ill.)
Motorcycle gangs
  A: 1: 123 (ill.)
Motorists
  PS: 179–80
Movies
  B: 51, 170, 175, 183
Muhammad, John Allen
  A: 2: 280–82
Murder. See also Serial killers
  Borden, Lizzie and, B: 24–30
  Bundy, Ted and, B: 31–38
  Capote, Truman and, B:
    41–42, 43
  contracted, B: 158–59
  degrees of, A: 1: 31; 2: 402
  homicide/murder distinction,
    A: 1: 61–62
  Kinkel, Kip and, A: 1: 61; B:
    111–19
  "Lawes Divine, Morall and
    Martiall," PS: 23

Loeb, Richard and Leopold,
    Nathan, PS: 118, 120–22
  manslaughter/murder distinc-
    tion, A: 1: 62–63
  McNaughtan, Daniel and, B:
    141–46
  media coverage of trials, A: 2:
    447–49
  Native Americans, A: 2: 336
  Sheppard, Sam and, B: 170–76
  street gangs, A: 1: 125
  Zantop, Susanne and Half, A:
    1: 59
Murder By Death
  B: 43–44
Murder mysteries
  A: 2: 444–45
Music download sites
  A: 1: 55
My Disillusionment in Russia
    (Goldman)
  B: 85

N

NAACP (National Association
    for the Advancement of
    Colored People)
  B: 6, 166
NAEC (North American Export
    Committee)
  A: 1: 86
Nairobi, Kenya
  A: 1: 181
Napster
  A: 1: 203 (ill.)
Naslund, Denise
  B: 35
National Advisory Commission
    on Civil Disorders
  A: 2: 257
National American Suffrage Al-
    liance
  B: 2
National Association for the Ad-
    vancement of Colored Peo-
    ple (NAACP)
  B: 6, 166
National Center for Missing and
    Exploited Children
  A: 2: 241
National Center for the Analysis
    of Violent Crime (NCAVC)
  B: 123

National Coalition Against Do-
    mestic Violence
  A: 2: 236
National Commission on Law
    Observance and Enforce-
    ment
  A: 1: 43
National Conference of Chari-
    ties and Correction
  B: 6
National Conference of Social
    Work
  B: 6
National Conference on Orga-
    nized Crime
  PS: 152
National crime commissions
  A: 2: 257–58
National Crime Victimization
    Survey (NCVS)
  A: 1: 73, 137; 2: 242, 413
National Cybercrime Training
    Partnership (NCTP)
  A: 1: 207
  PS: 199
National Equal Rights Party
  B: 127, 131
National Federation of Settle-
    ments
  B: 6–7
National Highway Traffic Safety
    Administration (NHTSA)
  A: 1: 138
National Institute of Justice
    (NIJ)
  A: 1: 141
National Insurance Crime Bu-
    reau (NICB)
  A: 1: 86
National Motor Vehicle Theft
    Act
  A: 1: 38, 42
National Organization for Vic-
    tim Assistance (NVOA)
  A: 2: 235–36
National political conventions
  B: 1–2
National Recovery Administra-
    tion (NRA)
  B: 51–52
National Strategy for Homeland
    Security
  A: 1: 185
  PS: 212

National University Law School
  B: 129–30
National Victim Center
  A: 2: 241
National White-Collar Crime
  Center (NW3C)
  A: 1: 207
National Woman's Suffrage As-
  sociation (NWSA)
  B: 136, 138 (ill.)
Nationalistic terrorism
  A: 1: 170–71
Native Americans, *PS:* 24
  colonists, relations with the,
    A: 1: 7
  crime statistics, *A:* 2: 422
  mediation, *A:* 2: 237
  Quakers, relations with the,
    A: 1: 6
  tribal justice, *A:* 2: 324,
    334–38
NCAVC (National Center for
  the Analysis of Violent
  Crime)
  B: 123
NCTP (National Cybercrime
  Training Partnership)
  A: 1: 207
NCVS (National Crime Victim-
  ization Survey)
  A: 1: 73, 137; 2: 242, 413
Nebraska
  PS: 117
Neglect
  A: 1: 70; 2: 354–55, 366
Negligence
  A: 1: 63
Neighborhood Watch. *See also*
  Community crime preven-
  tion
  A: 1: 53–54, 80; 2: 262
*Nellie Bly: Daredevil, Reporter,
  Feminist* (Kroeger)
  B: 82
Ness, Elliot (character)
  A: 2: 446
Netscape Communication
  PS: 142
Neurochemicals
  A: 1: 221
Nevada
  A: 1: 134
New Amsterdam
  A: 1: 4

New Deal
  A: 1: 104
  B: 50–51, 69
New England
  PS: 29–33, 33 (ill.), 35 (ill.)
New Hampshire
  PS: 116
"New Journalism"
  A: 2: 446
New Sweden
  A: 1: 4–5
New York, *B:* 53
  Auburn Prison, *A:* 1: 32 (ill.)
  Auburn prison plan, *A:* 1:
    32–33
  Centre Street Magistrates
    Court, *A:* 1: 13 (ill.)
  flexible sentencing, *A:* 2: 404
  Love Canal, *A:* 1: 150
  organized crime, *A:* 1: 119
  police force, *A:* 1: 34
  public executions, as first
    state to stop, *A:* 1: 31
  securities fraud, *A:* 1: 107
  settlement of, *A:* 1: 4
New York City Draft Riots
  of 1863
  B: 184, 187–89, 190 (ill.)
New York City police
  A: 2: 249, 252
  B: 184–91
New York Crime Commission
  PS: 71
New York Society for the Preven-
  tion of Cruelty to Children
  A: 2: 367
New York Stock Exchange
  A: 1: 106 (ill.)
New York Times
  Capote, Truman and, *B:* 41
  Goldman, Emma and, *B:* 82
  Haywood, William Dudley
    and, *B:* 85
  Kaczynski, Ted and, *B:* 102,
    103
New York World
  B: 82
New Yorker
  B: 41, 42
New York's Metropolitan Police
  Force
  B: 185–87, 186 (ill.), 189
New York's Municipal Police
  B: 185–87

New Zealand
  PS: 116
Newspapers, *PS:* 63. *See also* Me-
  dia
  Borden, Lizzie and, *B:* 28,
    29–30
  Dewey, Thomas E. and, *B:* 59
  Dickens, Charles and, *B:* 65–66
  Kaczynski, Ted and, *B:* 102, 103
  Sheppard, Sam and, *B:* 173–74
NHTSA (National Highway Traf-
  fic Safety Administration)
  A: 1: 138
NICB (National Insurance Crime
  Bureau)
  A: 1: 86
Nichols, Terry
  A: 1: 176, 181
NIJ (National Institute of Justice)
  A: 1: 141
9/11 Commission
  PS: 211
Nineteenth Amendment
  B: 132, 133, 137
Nineteenth century
  economic changes, *A:* 1:
    28–29
  juvenile justice, *A:* 2: 343
Nobel Peace Prize
  B: 1, 127
Nonfiction novels
  B: 39, 42–43
Norris, Clarence
  B: 162, 168–69
  PS: 160, 163, 170, 171
Norris, Donna Hagerman
  PS: 173, 174
Norris v. Alabama
  B: 165, 168
  PS: 163, 164
North American Export Com-
  mittee (NAEC)
  A: 1: 86
North Carolina
  A: 1: 5
Northern Ireland
  A: 1: 171
Northern Securities Company
  (NSC)
  PS: 140–41
Northern Securities Company v. U.S.
  PS: 141
Northern states
  PS: 171

Novelists. *See* Writers
Novels, nonfiction
   B: 39, 42–43
NRA (National Recovery Administration)
   B: 51–52
NSC (Northern Securities Company)
   PS: 140–41
Nuclear power plant accidents
   A: 1: 150
NW3C (National White-Collar Crime Center)
   A: 1: 207
NWSA (National Woman's Suffrage Association)
   B: 136, 138 (ill.)

O

Oath of allegiance
   B: 12
Obscenity. *See also* Pornography
   PS: 80–86
Occupational Safety and Health Act
   A: 1: 157
Ocean Dumping Act
   A: 1: 154
Odontology
   A: 2: 271–72
Offenders
   costs of crime, *A: 2:* 417
   mediation, *A: 2:* 237
   sex offenders, *A: 1:* 221; *2:* 364–65
Office of Child Support Enforcement, Justice Department
   A: 2: 374
Ohio
   A: 2: 448–49
Ohio River pollution
   A: 1: 153 (ill.)
Oil Pollution Act
   A: 1: 157
Oil spills
   A: 1: 149 (ill.), 150, 157, 163–65, 164 (ill.), 166
Oklahoma
   PS: 129
Oklahoma City bombing
   A: 1: 51, 176, 177 (ill.), 181

Olde Colonial Courthouse, Cape Cod
   A: 2: 290 (ill.)
Oliver Twist (Dickens)
   B: 63
Oliverson, Denise
   B: 35
O'Malley, Sean P.
   A: 2: 373
Omnibus Anti-Drug Abuse Act
   A: 2: 430–31
Omnibus Crime Control and Safe Streets Act
   A: 2: 259
On the Penitentiary System in the United States and Its Application to France (Beaumont, et al.)
   B: 10, 13, 14
Online auction fraud
   A: 1: 196 (ill.)
Online gambling
   A: 1: 199–200
Online pharmacies
   A: 1: 198–99
Operation Candy Box
   A: 1: 145–46
Operation Enduring Freedom
   PS: 208
Operation Green Quest
   PS: 205
Opium
   PS: 88–94, 89 (ill.), 93 (ill.), 96
Opium Exclusion Act of 1909
   PS: 89
Oregon State Penitentiary
   A: 2: 406 (ill.)
Oregon Trail
   B: 178
Orfila, Mathieu Joseph Bonaventura
   A: 2: 267
Organized crime, *B:* 53, 55, 57, 104–5, 107–9
   American Mafia, *PS:* 147–48, 148 (ill.), 153 (ill.), 153–54
   bootlegging, *A: 1:* 118; *PS:* 69, 99, 100, 150
   characteristics, *A: 1:* 116–17
   Commission, *A: 1:* 119, 120
   crime families, *A: 1:* 50, 111, 119, 120–21; *PS:* 148 (ill.), 153 (ill.), 153–54

crime syndicates, *A: 1:* 119
   definition, *PS:* 147
   drug trafficking, *A: 1:* 114; *PS:* 94, 96, 101
   entertainment industry, *A: 1:* 111
   federal law enforcement and, *A: 1:* 49–51
   fiction, *A: 2:* 446
   hazardous waste dumping, *A: 1:* 159
   international crime syndicates, *A: 1:* 128–29
   international organizations, *PS:* 154
   Internet gambling sites, *A: 1:* 200
   Kefauver committee, *A: 1:* 49
   labor racketeering, *A: 1:* 119–20
   legal businesses, *A: 1:* 115
   money laundering, *A: 1:* 114–15
   motorcycle gangs, *A: 1:* 122–23
   National Conference on Organized Crime, *PS:* 152
   pornography, *A: 1:* 116
   Prohibition and, *A: 1:* 42, 117–18; *PS:* 66
   prosecution, *A: 1:* 50–51
   Racketeer Influenced and Corrupt Organizations (RICO) Act, *A: 1:* 50–51; *PS:* 148–54
   street gangs, *A: 1:* 123–29
   white-collar crime, as distinct from, *PS:* 131, 133
Organized Crime Control Act of 1970. *See also* Racketeer Influenced and Corrupt Organizations (RICO) of 1970
   B: 105, 109
Organized Crime Section, FBI
   A: 1: 129
Organized labor
   Darrow, Clarence and, *B:* 48–49
   Haywood, William Dudley and, *B:* 84–85
   The Molly Maguires and, *B:* 158–59
   Pinkerton National Detective Agency and, *B:* 160

Walling, George Washington
and, *B: 190*
Original thirteen American
colonies
A: 1: 5 (ill.), 6
Ortiz, Antuilo Ramirez
A: 1: 184
Ortiz, David E.
A: 1: 166–67
Osborne, Sarah
PS: 35
Other Voices, Other Rooms
(Capote)
B: 41
Ott, Janice
B: 35
Overthrow of governments
PS: 218

P

Pacifism. *See* Peace
Page-jacking
A: 1: 195
Paint Unit, FBI
A: 2: 276
Palestine
A: 1: 182–83
Palestinian Liberation Front
A: 1: 180
Palmer, A. Mitchell
A: 1: 42
B: 90–91
Palmer Raids
A: 1: 42
B: 83, 90–91, 92
Pan American Airlines Flight
103
A: 1: 184
Pandering (Fleiss)
B: 182
Panic of 1893
B: 82
Paraphilia
A: 1: 134–35
Parens patriae
A: 2: 343, 361
Parental kidnappings
A: 2: 364
Parents of Murdered Children
A: 2: 236
Parents, responsibilities of
A: 2: 358, 360

Parker, Jimmy
A: 1: 59
Parks, Bernard
A: 2: 425 (ill.)
Parks, Roberta Kathleen
B: 35
Parole
A: 1: 33; *2:* 314–15, 315 (ill.),
399–400
Parole and probation
PS: 69, 72–73
Parris, Elizabeth
PS: 34–35, 36
Parris, Samuel
PS: 33–34, 40
Patent laws
A: 1: 55
Pathologist, FBI
A: 2: 265 (ill.)
Patriot Act. *See* USA Patriot Act
**"Patterns of Global Terror-
ism—2002"**
PS: 201–13
Patterson, Haywood
B: 162, 166–67, 167 (ill.), 168
PS: 160, 163, 165, 167, 169–71
Peace
B: 1, 2–3, 7, 8, 132
Pearl, Daniel
A: 1: 180
PS: 204
Pedophilia
A: 1: 135
Peel, Robert
A: 1: 34; *2:* 249
B: 143
"Peeping Tom"
B: 149
Peer influence and crime
A: 1: 222–23
Penal systems. *See* Prison reform
Penalties, antitrust
PS: 142–43
Penitentiary systems. *See* Prison
reform
Penn, William
A: 1: 5
Pennsylvania, *PS:* 198
capital punishment, *A: 2:*
401–2, 403
murder, first and second-
degree, *A: 1:* 31
police officer, *A: 1:* 206 (ill.)
prisons, *A: 1:* 30

settlement of, *A: 1:* 5–6
Pennsylvania prison plan
A: 1: 32–33
Pentagon
A: 1: 184
PS: 198
People Nations
A: 1: 127
"People's Charter"
B: 155–56
Personal adjustments in behav-
ior
A: 2: 415–16
Pesticides
A: 1: 148
Peterson, Laci
A: 2: 447
Peterson, Scott
A: 2: 447
Petit larceny
A: 1: 81–82
Pharmaceutical fraud
A: 1: 95–96
Pharmaceuticals. *See* Prescription
drugs
Pharmacies, online
A: 1: 198–99
Philadelphia
city hall, *A: 2:* 285 (ill.)
police, *A: 1:* 34
Philadelphia and Reading Coal
and Iron Company
B: 159
Philadelphia plan of corrections
PS: 56–63
Philadelphia Society for Alleviat-
ing the Miseries of Public
Prisons
A: 1: 30
Philadelphia System
B: 64, 65
Phosphorous waste
A: 1: 166
Photographic Unit, FBI
A: 2: 277
Physical abnormalities theories
of crime
A: 1: 212
Physical abuse
A: 1: 69–70
Physical anthropologists
A: 2: 272
Physical punishment
A: 1: 29

Pickpocketing
   A: 1: 76 (ill.), 77
The Pickwick Papers (Dickens)
   B: 63
Pilgrims
   A: 1: 2 (ill.)
Pillories
   A: 1: 17 (ill.)
Pimps
   A: 1: 134
Pinkerton, Allan
   B: **154–61,** 155 (ill.), 157 (ill.)
Pinkerton National Detective
   Agency
   A: 2: 250 (ill.), 252
   B: 154, 156–58, 159–60
"The Pinks." *See* Pinkerton Na-
   tional Detective Agency
Piracy
   A: 1: 203–5
Planning, computer use in
   A: 1: 195
Plantations
   A: 1: 5
Plea bargains
   A: 2: 236–37, 301–2
"Plea of Clarence Darrow"
   PS: **118–30**
Poe, Edgar Allan
   A: 2: 444
Poirot, Hercule (character)
   A: 2: 445
Poisoning, *A: 2:* 271
Police. *See also* Law enforcement
   Bureau of Indian Affairs, *A: 2:*
     335 (ill.)
   codes of ethics, *A: 2:* 394
   corruption, *A: 2:* 251
   counterterrorism, *A: 2:* 253
   military police, *A: 2:* 325 (ill.),
     327, 332 (ill.)
   minorities and, *A: 2:* 424–25
   racial profiling, *A: 2:* 425–27
   tribal, *A: 2:* 337 (ill.)
   women, *A: 1:* 35, 37
Police cars
   A: 2: 254 (ill.), 255
Policing
   advancements in, *A: 1:* 45
   challenges, *A: 2:* 262–63
   child support, *A: 2:* 374
   colonial period, *A: 1:* 14; *2:*
     246–48

   community policing, *A: 1:*
     54–55; *2:* 261 (ill.), 262
   cyber crime, *A: 1:* 205–8
   environmental law, *A: 1:*
     159–60
   federal, *A: 1:* 41
   guidelines, *A: 2:* 246
   jurisdictions, *B:* 156–57
   labor disputes, *B:* 160
   Law Enforcement Assistance
     Administration (LEAA), *A:*
     2: 258
   National Commission on Law
     Observance and Enforce-
     ment, *A: 1:* 43
   national crime commissions,
     A: 2: 257
   pornography, *A: 1:* 136–37
   professional policing, *A: 1:*
     33–36
   reform, *A: 2:* 252, 255
   searches, *A: 2:* 261–62
   suspects' rights, *A: 2:* 259–60
   tribal law enforcement agen-
     cies, *A: 2:* 337–38
   U. S. marshals, *A: 1:* 35, 35 (ill.)
   Walling, George Washington
     and, *B:* 184–91
Political cartoons
   Roosevelt, Theodore, *PS:* 141
     (ill.)
   Sherman Antitrust Act, *PS:*
     132 (ill.)
   Wickersham Law Enforcement
     Commission, *PS:* 68 (ill.)
Political conventions
   B: 1–2
Political questions
   A: 2: 287
Political trials
   B: 72–76
Political-social terrorism
   A: 1: 174–76
Politics. *See also* Radical politics
   Addams, Jane and, *B:* 1–2
   Bundy, Ted and, *B:* 32
   crime and, *A: 2:* 417
   Dewey, Thomas E. and, *B:*
     56–59
   France and, *B:* 11–12
   police and, *B:* 190–91
Population
   colonial period, *A: 2:* 23
   race/ethnicity, *A: 2:* 422

Pornography
   A: 1: 116, 132 (ill.), 135–37
   B: 178
   PS: 85
Porter, James
   A: 2: 370
Pory, John
   PS: 26
Postal Authority, U.S.
   PS: 81
Posters, wanted
   B: 160
Posttraumatic stress disorder
   A: 2: 389
Poverty
   B: 4–5
Powell, Colin
   PS: 211
Powell, Ozie
   B: 162, 169
   PS: 160, 168, 170, 171
Powell v. Alabama
   B: 166
   PS: 163
The Power of Sympathy (Brown)
   A: 2: 444
The Practice (TV show)
   A: 2: 447
Preliminary hearings
   A: 2: 301
Premeditation
   A: 1: 62–63
Prescription drugs
   A: 1: 95–96, 198–99
   B: 110, 112, 114, 115
   PS: 91–92
President's Commission on Law
   Enforcement and the Ad-
   ministration of Justice
   PS: 133
President's Task Force on Vic-
   tims of Crime
   A: 2: 236
Pretrial hearings
   A: 2: 331–32
Prevention of crime, *PS:* 71–72.
   See also Neighborhood
   Watch
   community efforts, *A: 1:* 54–55;
     2: 261 (ill.), 262, 413–15
   juvenile crime, *A: 1:* 57
   motor vehicle theft, *A: 1:* 87,
     87 (ill.)
   punishment, *A: 1:* 217–18

school violence, *A: 2:* 389–91, 390 (ill.)

shoplifting, *A: 1:* 82–84, 84 (ill.)

telemarketing fraud, *A: 1:* 101 (ill.)

Price, Victoria
  B: 164, 165, 167
  PS: 162, 163, 166, 168

Price-fixing
  A: 1: 108–9
  PS: 133, 134, 144

Principles of Criminology (Sutherland)
  A: 1: 214

Prison Fellowship Ministries
  A: 2: 398

Prison inmates
  PS: 52 (ill.)

Prison reform
  B: 10, 12–14, 64, 65

Prisoner isolation
  B: 64, 65

Prisoners
  classification, *PS:* 74
  mental capacity, *PS:* 72

Prisons
  Auburn plan, *A: 1:* 32–33
  boot camp prisons, *A: 2:* 310, 410 (ill.)
  colonial period, *A: 1:* 18
  construction, *A: 2:* 311–12
  crime prevention, *A: 2:* 415
  education, *A: 1:* 215, 216 (ill.)
  famous, *A: 2:* 308–9
  federal, *A: 1:* 41
  incarceration rates, *A: 2:* 428, 432
  juvenile, *A: 2:* 348 (ill.)
  middle ages, *A: 2:* 393
  Pennsylvania, *A: 1:* 30, 32–33
  population, *A: 1:* 46–47; *2:* 310–11
  prison industries, *A: 1:* 32, 48–49
  prisoners, *A: 1:* 210 (ill.)
  race/ethnicity, *A: 2:* 429–30
  rehabilitation, *A: 1:* 49
  religion in, *A: 2:* 396–98
  silence, *A: 1:* 31
  southern states, *A: 1:* 33
  state prisons, *A: 1:* 30–31
  supermax prisons, *A: 2:* 312–13

treatment of prisoners, *A: 1:* 48–49

women, *A: 1:* 42; *2:* 316–17

Privacy
  A: 2: 352–53

Private health insurance fraud
  A: 1: 95–96

Private industry
  PS: 194, 195

Private investigators
  B: 154–61

Private police
  A: 2: 251–52

Private prisons
  A: 1: 47; *2:* 309–10

Private security firms
  A: 2: 260–61

Probation
  A: 1: 33; *2:* 35, 306–8, 352, 430

Probation and parole
  PS: 69, 72–73

The Problem of Law Enforcement
  PS: 66–75

Proceedings
  antitrust, *PS:* 139
  Racketeer Influenced and Corrupt Organizations (RICO) Act, *PS:* 152

Professional criminals
  arsonists, *A: 1:* 88–89
  burglars, *A: 1:* 79
  car thieves, *A: 1:* 86
  thieves, *A: 1:* 77

Professional police
  A: 2: 249–51

Professional victim advocates
  A: 2: 240–41

Profiling, criminal
  B: 123

Progressive Movement
  A: 1: 213

Prohibition, *A: 1:* 39, 42, 117–18; *2:* 253; *B:* 55, 56, 179
  bootlegging, *PS:* 150
  Commission on Law Observance and Enforcement, *PS:* 67
  Eighteenth Amendment, *PS:* 79, 99–100
  organized crime and, *PS:* 66, 133

"Pro-Life" activists. *See* Antiabortion activists

Property crimes
  motivation, *A: 1:* 75, 77
  new laws, *A: 1:* 29
  rise in levels of, *A: 1:* 53
  types of, *A: 1:* 75, 77–78

Property, forfeiture of
  drug crimes, *PS:* 95
  Racketeer Influenced and Corrupt Organizations (RICO) Act, *PS:* 151
  Sherman Antitrust Act, *PS:* 139

Prosecution
  rape, *A: 1:* 72
  white-collar crime, *A: 1:* 94

Prosecutorial Remedies and Other Tools to End the Exploitation of Children Today Act. *See* PROTECT Act of 2003

Prosecutors
  A: 1: 19; *2:* 298
  B: 28, 29, 53, 55, 56–57

Prostitution
  A: 1: 115–16, 131, 133–34
  B: 178–81, 181 (ill.), 183
  PS: 86

PROTECT Act of 2003
  A: 2: 365
  PS: 173–83

Protests
  Civil Rights Movement, *B:* 95
  Frankfurter, Felix and, *B:* 74–76
  Scottsboro Boys and, *B:* 167–68, 167 (ill.)

Protests and demonstrations
  capital punishment, *A: 2:* 404 (ill.)
  racial profiling, *A: 2:* 420 (ill.)

Psychological disorders theories crime
  A: 1: 213

Psychological harm of solitary confinement
  PS: 58–63

Psychological profiling
  B: 123

Psychopathy
  A: 1: 213

Public defenders
  A: 2: 299, 300 (ill.)
Public executions
  A: 1: 29, 31
Public hangings
  A: 2: 406
Public intoxication
  PS: 101
Public order crimes. *See also*
  Moral offenses
  abnormal sexual behavior, *A:*
  1: 134–35
  driving under the influence
  (DUI), *A: 1:* 138–39
  drugs, *A: 1:* 140–46
  pornography, *A: 1:* 135–37
  prostitution, *A: 1:* 133–34
Public schools
  A: 2: 362
Publicity. *See* Media
Punishment. *See also* Capital
  punishment; Corrections
  colonial period, *A: 1:* 15,
  16 18; *2:* 392, 395
  as deterrent, *A: 1:* 217–18
  effect on crime, *PS:* 125
  environmental crime, *A: 1:*
  159–60
  Europe, *A: 2:* 392, 394
  prisons, *A: 1:* 30–33
  robbery, *A: 1:* 66
  sentences for drug offenses,
  PS: 95–96
Purchasing of weapons
  PS: 223–24
Pure Food and Drug Law
  PS: 88–89
Puritans
  A: 1: 4, 14, 15 (ill.)
  PS: 29–33
Putnam, Ann
  PS: 36, 39

Q

Quakers
  A: 1: 5–6; *2:* 403
Questioned Documents
  A: 2: 270
Questioned Documents Unit, FBI
  A: 2: 276, 282
Quimby, George P.
  PS: 112

R

Race riots
  A: 1: 55; *2:* 257
Race/ethnicity. *See also* specific
  groups
  causes of minority crime
  rates, *A: 2:* 435
  crime, effects of, *A: 2:* 416
  diversity, *A: 2:* 419, 421
  hate crimes, *A: 2:* 433–35
  murder, *A: 1:* 64
  racial profiling, *A: 2:* 425–27
  rape, *A: 1:* 73–76
  sentencing, *A: 2:* 427–28
  violence in minority commu-
  nities, *A: 2:* 432–33
  War on Drugs, *A: 2:* 430–32
Racial profiling
  A: 2: 420 (ill.), 425–27, 426
  (ill.)
Racial segregation
  B: 69
Racial tensions
  B: 189
Racketeer Influenced and Cor-
  rupt Organization (RICO)
  Act of 1970
  A: 1: 50–51, 113–14, 121–22
  B: 105, 109
  PS: 147–55
Racketeering. *See also* Organized
  crime
  B: 20–21, 108
Radical politics
  B: 78–79, 80, 81–84, 87, 90–92
Railroads
  B: 156–57, 162–64
  PS: 140–41
Rake's Progress: Scene at Bedlam
  (Hogarth)
  B: 144 (ill.)
Raleigh, Sir Walter
  A: 1: 3
Ramsey, Evan
  A: 2: 382–83
Rancourt, Susan Elaine
  B: 35
Random House
  B: 41, 42
Ransom
  A: 2: 364
Rape
  A: 1: 70–74; *2:* 232, 233, 233
  (ill.), 234

B: 149–50, 152–53, 162–69,
  163 (ill.)
Rapp, Lou
  B: 180
Rappe, Virginia
  A: 2: 439
"Rat Pack"
  A: 1: 117
RCRA (Resource Conservation
  and Recovery Act)
  A: 1: 154–56
Readings, Dickens, Charles and
  B: 66
Reagan, Ronald
  B: 123, 143
  PS: 95
Real Irish Republican Army
  (RIRA)
  A: 1: 171
Reasonable business practices
  PS: 144
Rebellion, Stamp Act
  A: 1: 24 (ill.)
Records, access to
  PS: 206, 207
Records of juveniles
  A: 2: 345, 352–53
Recruitment, terrorist
  PS: 229–30
"Red Emma." *See* Goldman,
  Emma
"Red Queen of Anarchy." *See*
  Goldman, Emma
Red Scare
  A: 1: 42
  B: 72, 90
Redress
  PS: 10–11
Reese, Marilyn. *See* Sheppard,
  Marilyn
Reform
  criminal justice system, *A:*
  1: 29
  juvenile justice, *A: 1:* 56;
  2: 343
  legal system, *A: 1:* 21
  policing, *A: 2:* 255; *PS:* 75
  prison reform, *A: 1:* 30
  rape laws, *A: 1:* 72
  social, *PS:* 63
Reform facilities
  A: 2: 351
Reformed death row prisoners
  A: 2: 314

Reformers, social. *See* Social activists

Regional AMBER Alert plans
  PS: 181

Registration
  narcotics dealers, *PS:* 90–91
  sex offenders, *A: 2:* 365; *PS:* 182

Regulation of securities
  A: 1: 104–5

Regulations, environmental
  A: 1: 158

Regulations, handguns
  B: 115

Rehabilitation
  A: 1: 30, 49, 211

Reid, Richard
  PS: 204

Reilly, Tom
  PS: 142

Release from prison
  PS: 61–62

Reliefs. *See* Taxes

Religion
  colonial period, *A: 1:* 8, 14–16; *2:* 392
  crime prevention, *A: 2:* 407
  European punishment, role in, *A: 2:* 392, 396
  freedom of, *A: 1:* 5–6
  terrorism, *A: 1:* 171–73

Religious issues
  church attendance, *PS:* 22–23
  divine power of kings, *PS:* 17–18

Religious Land Use and Institutionalized Persons Act
  A: 2: 398

Remove Intoxicated Drivers (RID)
  A: 1: 138

Reno v. ACLU
  A: 1: 136

Repeal of the Eighteenth Amendment
  PS: 101, 101 (ill.)

Repeat offenders
  A: 1: 73

Repentance
  A: 1: 13

Reporting
  child abuse, *A: 2:* 367–68
  rape, *A: 1:* 73
  rape victims, *A: 2:* 233–34

Republican form of government
  A: 1: 20

Republicans
  B: 32, 56, 57, 59

Residential centers
  A: 2: 319 (ill.), 320

Resource Conservation and Recovery Act (RCRA)
  A: 1: 154–56

Ressler, Robert
  B: 123

Restitution
  A: 2: 231, 234

Restorative justice
  A: 2: 347

Restraint of trade or commerce
  PS: 138

Retail stores
  A: 1: 79, 82–83, 84 (ill.)

The Revolution
  B: 136

Revolutionary War
  A: 1: 1, 20, 21, 25

Rewards
  A: 1: 187 (ill.)
  PS: 205

Rhode Island
  A: 1: 31

Rhodia, Inc.
  A: 1: 167

Ricin
  A: 1: 182

RICO. *See* Racketeer Influenced and Corrupt Organization (RICO) Act of 1970

Ridge, Tom
  PS: 197 (ill.)

Rifling studies
  A: 2: 268

Riots
  A: 1: 24 (ill.); *2:* 257, 258 (ill.), 425

RIRA (Real Irish Republican Army)
  A: 1: 171

Roach, Joe
  A: 2: 367

Roadblock
  A: 1: 138 (ill.)

Roanoke Island
  A: 1: 3

Robbery
  A: 1: 45, 65–68
  B: 148–50

Roberson, Willie
  B: 162, 169
  PS: 168, 170–71

Robinson, George D.
  B: 29

Rockefeller, John D.
  PS: 135

Rockefeller, Nelson
  B: 32

Rockford Female Seminary
  B: 3

Rodney King riots
  A: 1: 55; *2:* 425

Rolfe, John
  PS: 26

Roman Catholic Church
  PS: 86

Rome, Italy
  PS: 209 (ill.)

Roosevelt, Eleanor
  PS: 14

Roosevelt, Franklin D.
  A: 1: 45
  B: 50–51, 56, 76
  PS: 100–1

Roosevelt, Theodore
  A: 2: 252
  B: 2, 28
  PS: 140–41, 141 (ill.)

Rouse, Jamie
  A: 2: 381

Roving wiretaps
  PS: 206, 207

Rule, Ann
  A: 2: 446

Runnymede, England
  PS: 1, 7, 15

Russia
  B: 80, 84–85

Rwanda
  A: 2: 297

S

Sabbath
  PS: 23

Sacco, Nicola
  B: 72–76, 73 (ill.)

SACs (Security assessment centers)
  PS: 195

Sadomasochism
  A: 1: 135

Salem Witch Trials
  A: 1: 10
  PS: 4, 30 (ill.), 33–40
San Francisco, California
  PS: 90
San Francisco Madam
  B: 177, 180–81, 183
San Quentin State Prison
  A: 2: 308–9, 313 (ill.)
Sandys, Sir Edwin
  PS: 26
Sanger, Margaret
  PS: 83–84, 84 (ill.), 85
Sanity test
  B: 141
Santa Barbara, California
  A: 1: 150
Sarin nerve gas
  A: 1: 182
Sausalito
  B: 183
Savings and loan industry collapse
  A: 1: 52, 97
The Scarlet Letter (Hawthorne)
  A: 1: 16
Schall v. Martin
  A: 2: 347–48
Scheck, Barry
  A: 2: 449
School shootings
  A: 1: 57, 61, 65; *2:* 378–86, 379 (ill.)
School violence
  B: 111, 114–15, 116
School violence prevention
  A: 2: 389–91
Scopes, John T.
  B: 48 (ill.), 49, 50–51
Scopes trial
  B: 48 (ill.), 49, 50–51
Scottsboro Boys
  B: **162–69**, 163 (ill.), 165 (ill.)
  PS: 161 (ill.)
"Scottsboro Case Goes to the Jury"
  PS: **160–72**
SDS (Students for a Democratic Society)
  A: 1: 174–75, 175 (ill.)
Search warrants
  PS: 206

Searches and seizures
  "exclusionary rule," *A: 2:* 259–60
  Fourth Amendment, *A: 1:* 27; *2:* 248
  illegal, *B:* 75
  military justice, *A: 2:* 332
  Prohibition, *A: 1:* 42
  relaxation of rules, *A: 2:* 261–62
SEC. *See* Security Exchange Commission (SEC)
Secret Service
  A: 2: 250–51
Secret service agencies. *See* Pinkerton National Detective Agency
Securities Act
  A: 1: 104, 202
Securities and Exchange Commission (SEC)
  A: 1: 104–5, 202
Securities Exchange Act
  A: 1: 104, 202
Securities fraud
  A: 1: 103–7, 201–2
  B: 21
Security
  personal adjustments in behavior, *A: 2:* 415–16
  at schools, *A: 2:* 389–90, 390 (ill.)
  shoplifting prevention, *A: 1:* 82–83
Security assessment centers (SACs)
  PS: 195
Security Exchange Commission (SEC)
  A: 1: 104–5, 202
  B: 19, 20–21, 22–23
Security guard
  A: 1: 84 (ill.)
Sedition
  A: 1: 42
Sedition Act of 1918
  B: 91
Segregation
  A: 2: 422
  B: 69
  PS: 157, 158
Self-defense
  A: 1: 61–62, 63; *2:* 416 (ill.)

Self-incrimination
  A: 1: 27
  B: 147, 149–50, 151
Senate Crime Investigating Committee
  A: 1: 49, 50 (ill.)
Senate Subcommittee on Antitrust and Monopoly
  B: 110
Senate Subcommittee on Investigations
  A: 1: 120
Sentencing
  capital punishment, *A: 2:* 404–5
  crime family bosses, *A: 1:* 121–22
  and crime prevention, *A: 1:* 218
  drug laws, *PS:* 95
  factors in, *A: 2:* 304, 306
  growing prison population, *A: 2:* 310–11
  guidelines, *A: 2:* 428
  juvenile courts, *A: 2:* 351–52
  Kemmler, William, *PS:* 106
  Loeb, Richard and Leopold, Nathan, *PS:* 128–29
  military justice, *A: 2:* 332–33
  organized crime, *PS:* 154
  Patterson, Haywood, *PS:* 169–70
  prison population and, *A: 1:* 47
  process, *A: 2:* 302
  race/ethnicity, *A: 2:* 427–28
  Scottsboro Boys, *PS:* 162, 163, 169–70
Separate System
  B: 64, 65
  PS: 56–63
September 11th attacks
  A: 1: 51, 169 (ill.), 183, 184; *2:* 253
  PS: 184, 185 (ill.), 198, 230
Serial killers
  B: 31–38, 123
Serial murder
  A: 1: 65
Serotonin
  A: 1: 221
Settlements, lawsuit
  Catholic Church, *A: 2:* 373
  Colonial Pipeline Company, *A: 1:* 166

Exxon Mobil Corporation, *A: 1:* 164–65
General Motors Corporation, *A: 1:* 163
Microsoft, *PS:* 142–43
Tyson Foods, *A: 1:* 165
Wal-Mart, *A: 1:* 163
Settlers
  A: 1: 3–6
Sex offender registration
  PS: 182
Sex offenders
  A: 1: 221; *2:* 364–65
Sexual abuse. *See* Child sexual
  abuse
Sexual crimes
  PS: 24
Sexual Homicide: Patterns and Motives (Ressler)
  B: 123
Sexual offenses
  A: 1: 134–35
"The Shadow" (radio program)
  A: 2: 445
Shakespeare, William
  B: 142
Shame penalties
  A: 2: 395
Sheikh, Saeed
  A: 1: 180
Sheppard, Marilyn
  B: 170, 171, 172, 173 (ill.)
Sheppard, Sam
  A: 2: 443
  B: 170–76, 171 (ill.)
Sheriffs
  A: 1: 14; *2:* 246–47
Sherman Antitrust Act of 1890
  A: 1: 109
  PS: 134–46
"Shield laws"
  A: 1: 72
Shoplifting
  A: 1: 82–83
Siegel, Bugsy
  A: 1: 117
Signs, changeable message
  PS: 180
Silent Spring (Carson)
  A: 1: 148
Silent System
  B: 64
  PS: 56, 58

Simpson, Nicole Brown
  A: 2: 448, 449
Simpson, O. J.
  A: 2: 425, 438 (ill.), 447,
    448–49, 449 (ill.)
Sing Sing Prison
  A: 1: 48; *2:* 309
  B: 13
  PS: 115
Sison, José Maria
  PS: 205
Slavery, *B:* 47, 136, 158–59;
  PS: 54
  capital punishment, *A: 2:* 403
  colonial period, *A: 1:* 18–19
  overview, *A: 1:* 36; *2:* 421
  slave patrols, *A: 2:* 247, 424
  whipping, *A: 1:* 33
Smart, Ed
  PS: 173
Smart, Elizabeth
  PS: 173
Smith, John
  PS: 18–19, 19 (ill.)
Smith, Melissa
  B: 35
Smith, Perry, tombstone
  B: 44 (ill.)
Smith, Susan
  A: 2: 368
Sniper attacks
  A: 2: 280–82
Snitches
  A: 1: 82
Snyder, LeRoy
  B: 178
Social activists
  Addams, Jane, *B:* 1–9
  Dickens, Charles, *B:* 61–68
  Goldman, Emma, *B:* 78–86
  Mansfield, Arabella, *B:* 134–40
Social affects of crime
  A: 2: 416–17
Social order
  A: 1: 14
Social reform
  A: 2: 343
  PS: 63
Social settlements
  B: 4–5
Social theories of crime
  A: 1: 213–14
Socialism
  B: 8

Socialist Party of America
  B: 84
Sociopathy
  A: 1: 213
Solitary confinement
  B: 64, 65
  PS: 56–63
Solomon, Anthony
  A: 2: 385
Son of Sam laws
  A: 2: 234
The Sopranos (TV show)
  A: 1: 111
South Carolina
  A: 1: 5
Southern colonies
  A: 2: 247
Southern states, *PS:* 156, 158,
  171
  African Americans, *A: 1:* 33
  black Americans, *A: 1:* 36
  Black Codes, *A: 1:* 5, 36; *2:*
    421
  Jim Crow laws, *A: 2:* 422
  prisons, *A: 1:* 33
Soviet Union
  B: 80, 84–85
  PS: 116
Spagnoli, Ernest
  B: 179
Special Committee on Organized Crime in Interstate Commerce. *See* Kefauver Committee
Special court-martials
  A: 2: 330
"Speech by Louis J. Freeh"
  PS: 188–200
Speech, freedom of
  A: 2: 374
"Speedy." *See* Hoover, J. Edgar
Speedy public trials, right to
  A: 1: 28
  PS: 49–50, 51
Spencer, Brenda
  A: 2: 381
Spitzer, Eliot
  A: 1: 107
Spitzka, Edward Charles
  PS: 112, 113
Spouse abuse. *See* Domestic violence
Springer, Francis
  B: 138

Spying
  B: 157, 158
  PS: 225–28
Stalking
  A: 1: 71
Stamp Act
  A: 1: 24
Standard & Poor's
  B: 20
Standard Oil Company
  PS: 135, 136, 141
*Standard Oil of New Jersey v.
  United States*
  PS: 135
Stanford, Sally
  B: **177–83**
Stanton, Elizabeth Cady
  B: 136
Starr, Ellen Gates
  B: 4–5
State courts
  appellate courts, *A: 2:* 293
  domestic violence courts, *A:
    2:* 296–98
  drug courts, *A: 2:* 295–96
  federal courts and, *A: 2:* 284,
    286
  judges, *A: 2:* 292–94
  jurisdiction, *A: 2:* 287
  lower courts, *A: 2:* 292
  role of, *A: 2:* 288, 291–92
  supreme courts, *A: 2:* 293
  trial courts, *A: 2:* 292–93
State police
  A: 1: 37; *2:* 256
State prisons
  A: 1: 30–31, 46; *2:* 308–9
State sponsored terrorism
  A: 1: 173–74, 187
State v. (TV show)
  A: 2: 449
States
  AMBER Alert, *PS:* 175, 179–81
  capital punishment, *A: 2:*
    404–5
  child protective services, *A: 2:*
    368–69
  child support enforcement, *A:
    2:* 374
  crime and punishment, re-
    sponsibility for, *A: 1:* 25
  criminal justice, responsibility
    for, *A: 1:* 41

cyber crime jurisdiction, *A: 1:*
  205–6
drug laws, *PS:* 95
electrocution, *PS:* 116
environmental laws, *A: 1:* 160
juvenile justice, *A: 1:* 56–57;
  2: 294–95, 345
powers of state governments,
  PS: 53
state police, *A: 1:* 37; *2:* 256
victims' bill of rights, *A: 2:*
  236–37
victims' compensation funds,
  A: 2: 235
Statistics
  aggravated assault, *A: 1:*
    68–69
  alcohol and crime, *A: 1:* 137
  alcohol related vehicle acci-
    dents, *A: 1:* 138
  annual cost of crime, *A: 2:*
    411
  arson, *A: 1:* 90
  Asian Americans and crime,
    A: 2: 431
  burglary, *A: 1:* 80–81
  capital punishment, *A: 2:* 400,
    428–29; *PS:* 116–17, 129
  child protective services, *A: 2:*
    369
  colonial criminals, *A: 1:* 18
  Colonial Pipeline Company
    oil spills, effects of the, *A:
    1:* 166
  costs of crime, *A: 2:* 411,
    412–13
  crime rates, *A: 2:* 378
  crime victims, *A: 2:* 229
  death row, *A: 2:* 313
  district court cases, *A: 2:* 290
  drug use, *A: 1:* 142
  Exxon Valdez oil spill, effects
    of the, *A: 1:* 164
  firearms and crime, *A: 1:* 224
  firearms in schools, *A: 2:*
    388–89
  forcible rape, *A: 1:* 73–74
  hate crimes, *A: 1:* 62; *2:* 433
  Homeland Security Depart-
    ment, cost of the, *A: 2:* 417
  incarceration rates by
    race/ethnicity, *A: 2:* 428,
    429–30
  juvenile crime, *A: 2:* 344

larceny-theft, *A: 1:* 84–85
minority crime rates, *A: 2:*
  435
motor vehicle theft, *A: 1:*
  87–88
murder, *A: 1:* 63–64
Native Americans and crime,
  A: 2: 422
need for crime statistics, *PS:*
  70, 74
parole, *A: 2:* 314
population and race/ethnicity,
  A: 2: 422
prison construction costs, *A:
  2:* 311
prison population, *A: 2:*
  310–11
prisoners, *A: 1:* 46–47
probation, *A: 2:* 306
property crimes, *A: 1:* 77–78
rape victims, *A: 2:* 233
repeat offenders, *A: 2:* 407
robbery, *A: 1:* 66–68
Salem Witch Trials, *PS:* 39
sources of, *A: 2:* 242
street gangs, *A: 1:* 125–26, 127
tribal law enforcement agen-
  cies, *A: 2:* 337–38
women in prison, *A: 2:* 316
Status offenses
  A: 2: 344
Statutory rape
  A: 1: 70
Stealing
  PS: 23, 25
Stenographic machine
  A: 2: 293 (ill.)
Steunenberg, Frank
  B: 84
Stevenson, Adlai
  B: 110
Stewart, Martha
  A: 1: 53, 106, 107 (ill.)
Stimson, Henry
  B: 71
Stock fraud. See Securities fraud
Stocks, trading
  B: 18–19, 22
Stolen property
  A: 1: 79
Stone, Oliver
  B: 23
"Stop Family Violence" stamp
  A: 1: 69 (ill.)

Storage of unlawfully obtained information
A: 1: 195
Storage of weapons
PS: 225
Storm water violations
A: 1: 162–63
Stoughton, William
PS: 40
Street gangs
A: 1: 119, 123–29, 127 (ill.);
2: 381, 388, 431
Streetwalkers
A: 1: 133–34, 134 (ill.)
Structural Design Unit, FBI
A: 2: 279, 282
Students Against Destructive De-
cisions (SADD)
A: 1: 138
Students for a Democratic Soci-
ety (SDS)
A: 1: 174–75, 175 (ill.)
Studies
cost of crime, A: 2: 411
victims, A: 2: 241–43
Substance abuse
A: 1: 224
Suicide bombings
A: 1: 181–83
Summary court-martials
A: 2: 329
Sunday laws
A: 1: 16
Superfund Amendments and
Reauthorization Act
A: 1: 156–57
Supermax prisons
A: 2: 312–13
Supreme Court, A: 2: 291 (ill.)
Bill of Rights and military
personnel, A: 2: 328–29
black Americans, ruling con-
cerning, A: 1: 36
cameras in the courtroom, A:
2: 442–44
capital punishment, A: 2: 404,
405
juvenile justice rulings, A: 2:
294–95, 347–48, 353
Philadelphia city hall, A: 2:
285 (ill.)
prosecution, rulings favoring,
A: 2: 261
racial profiling, A: 2: 427

role of, A: 2: 291
"shield laws," A: 1: 72
suspects' rights, A: 2: 259–60
Surveillance, detecting
PS: 228
Suspects' rights
A: 2: 259–60
Sutherland, Edwin
A: 1: 92, 214–15
Sweden
PS: 192
Swedish colonists
A: 1: 4–5

T

Taft, William H.
PS: 141
"Taking the Fifth"
B: 104
Taliban
A: 1: 185
PS: 203, 208
Tandy, Karen
A: 1: 145
Targets
of professional burglars, A: 1:
79–81
of robbery, A: 1: 67
of terrorism, PS: 214–15, 218,
228–29
Tax evasion
B: 56, 57
Tax fraud
A: 1: 42
Taxes
feudal, England, PS: 6–7, 10
first tax in America, PS: 27
liquor, PS: 99
narcotics, PS: 89, 90
Taylor, Francis X.
PS: 202
TEA-21 (Transportation Equity
Act for the Twenty-First
Century)
A: 1: 140
Technology, police
A: 2: 255
Teenagers
A: 1: 70
Telemarketing fraud
A: 1: 100–2
Television, B: 42, 170, 175, 183.
See also Media

legal dramas, A: 2: 447, 450
mystery shows, A: 2: 445–46
"Tender years" policy
A: 2: 361
Tennessee
A: 2: 404
Tennessee Supreme Court
B: 51
Terrorism
airlines, A: 1: 184–85
anti-U.S. attacks, PS: 231
assassinations, A: 1: 179–80
bases of operations, PS:
220–21
bombings, A: 1: 180–83
chemical and biological, A: 1:
182–83
communication and trans-
portation, PS: 222–23
computer use by terrorists,
PS: 193
cost of, A: 2: 417
counterterrorism measures, A:
1: 51–52
definition, A: 1: 168
environmental terrorism, A:
1: 177–78
espionage and information
gathering, PS: 225–28
individual terrorism, A: 1:
178–79
kidnappings, A: 1: 179–80
material support of, PS: 207
nationalistic, A: 1: 170–71
political-social terrorism, A: 1:
174–76
recruitment, PS: 229–30
religious terrorism, A: 1:
171–73
September 11th attacks, A: 1:
51
State Department report on,
excerpt from, PS: 201–5,
208–10
state-sponsored, A: 1: 173–74
targets, PS: 214–15, 218,
227–29
terrorist groups, PS: 204, 205,
231
USA Patriot Act, A: 1: 51,
187–88; 2: 253
weapons, PS: 223–25
weapons of mass destruction,
PS: 212

Terrorist Financing Task Force
  PS: 205
Terrorist lists
  A: 1: 187–89
Terrorist Threat Integration Center (TTIC)
  A: 1: 186
  PS: 198
Terrorists, Kaczynski, Ted
  B: 97–103
Testosterone
  A: 1: 221
Texas
  PS: 116, 129
Texas Rangers
  A: 2: 256
Thayer, James Bradley
  B: 71
Theft
  A: 1: 75, 194, 202–3
Then It All Came Down (Capote)
  B: 43
Theory of evolution. *See* Scopes trial
Thirteenth Amendment
  A: 1: 36
Thomas E. Dewey on the Two Party System (Dewey)
  B: 59
Three Mile Island nuclear power plant accident
  A: 1: 150
"Three strikes" laws
  A: 1: 73; *2:* 433
Thurston High School
  B: 111, 114–17
Tindal, Nicholas
  B: 141
Tires, dumping of
  A: 1: 161–62
Tituba
  PS: 35
Tobacco
  A: 1: 4
  PS: 26, 94–95
Tocqueville, Alexis de
  A: 1: 31
  B: 10, 11–15, 12 (ill.)
Tokyo, Japan
  A: 1: 182
Tombstones
  B: 44 (ill.)
Toolmark identification
  A: 2: 268, 269 (ill.)

Tools, borrowing
  PS: 24
Touting
  A: 1: 201–2
Toxicology
  A: 2: 267, 270–71, 276
  B: 122
Toynbee Hall
  B: 4
Trace evidence
  A: 2: 271–72, 272 (ill.)
  B: 122
Trace Evidence Unit, FBI
  A: 2: 282
Trade secrets
  A: 1: 202–4
  PS: 195
Trademark laws
  A: 1: 55
Trading. *See* Insider trading
Traffic stops
  A: 2: 426–27
Training
  law enforcement, *A: 1:* 45
  police, *A: 2:* 255
  prison chaplains, *A: 2:* 397
Training camps, Al Qaeda
  PS: 227 (ill.)
Transportation, Department of
  PS: 177, 179
Transportation Equity Act for the Twenty-First Century (TEA-21)
  A: 1: 140
Transportation plans, terrorists'
  PS: 223, 224–25
Treason
  A: 1: 25
Treatment, substance abuse
  A: 1: 224; *2:* 296
Trial by jury. *See also* Juries; "Amendments to the Constitution," *PS:* 50
  Bill of Rights, *PS:* 51
  Magna Carta, basis in the, *PS:* 10, 13
Trial courts
  A: 2: 292–93
Trials
  Borden, Lizzie, *B:* 27–30
  Flegenheimer, Arthur, *B:* 57
  Haymarket, *B:* 81
  McNaughtan, Daniel and, *B:* 144–45

political, *B:* 72–76
Scopes, John T., *B:* 48 (ill.), 49, 50–51
Scottsboro Boys, *B:* 164, 166, 168–69
Sheppard, Sam, *B:* 173–75
Tribal Courts Program
  A: 2: 338
Tribal justice
  A: 2: 237, 324, 334–38
True crime
  A: 2: 446
  B: 42–43
True Sun
  B: 63
Truman, Bess
  B: 57
Truman, Harry S.
  B: 57–59, 58 (ill.), 93
Trusts
  A: 1: 109
  PS: 135–36, 138
TTIC (Terrorist Threat Integration Center)
  A: 1: 186
Tubbs, David
  A: 1: 95 (ill.)
Tulloch, Robert
  A: 1: 59
Twenty-first Amendment
  PS: 101
"Two strikes" rule
  A: 2: 365
Two-way radios
  A: 2: 254 (ill.), 255
Tyson Foods
  A: 1: 165

U

UCMJ (Uniform Code of Military Justice)
  A: 2: 328, 333
UCR (Uniform Crime Report)
  A: 1: 43; *2:* 242
  PS: 74
UNABOM
  B: 101
"Unabomber." *See also* Kaczynski, Ted
  A: 1: 51, 179, 179 (ill.); *2:* 279
"Unabomber Manifesto" (Kaczynski)
  B: 97, 103

Underground Railroad
  B: 47, 159
Unemployment and crime
  A: 1: 214–15, 217
  PS: 71
Uniform Child Custody Jurisdiction Act
  A: 2: 364
Uniform Code of Military Justice (UCMJ)
  A: 2: 328, 333
Uniform Crime Report (UCR)
  A: 1: 43; *2:* 242
  PS: 74
Uniform Interstate Family Support Act
  A: 2: 374
Uniforms, police
  A: 1: 34
United Nations
  A: 2: 297
  PS: 205
United States. *See also* specific agencies and departments
  de Beaumont, Gustave and, *B:* 13–15
  de Tocqueville, Alexis and, *B:* 13–15
  Dickens, Charles and, *B:* 63–64, 65, 66–68
  Europeans and, *B:* 10
  World War I, *B:* 90
Uniting and Strengthening America by Providing Appropriate Tools Required to Intercept and Obstruct Terrorism Act. *See* USA Patriot Act
Universal Declaration of Human Rights
  PS: 14
Universal Franchise Association
  B: 129
Universal Peace Union (UPU)
  B: 132
Unlawful debts, collection of
  PS: 150
Unlawful entry
  A: 1: 78
Unreasonable searches and seizures, protection from. *See also* Searches and seizures
  PS: 49, 51

Unreformed death row prisoners
  A: 2: 314
The Untouchables (TV show)
  A: 2: 446
Urban decay
  A: 2: 414 (ill.)
U.S. attorneys
  A: 2: 287, 290
U.S. Communist Party
  B: 92, 110, 166
U.S. Congress
  Hoover, J. Edgar and, *B:* 95
  Lockwood, Belva Ann and, *B:* 130
  organized crime and, *B:* 107–9
  vices and, *B:* 179
U.S. Constitution
  B: 74
U.S. Court of Claims
  B: 130
U.S. Department of Justice (DOJ)
  B: 90–91
U.S. Embassy bombings
  A: 1: 181
U.S. marshals
  A: 1: 35, 35 (ill.); *2:* 248, 250, 255, 287, 290
U.S. Senate
  B: 95, 104–10, 107 (ill.)
U.S. Supreme Court, *A: 1:* 26; *B:* 74–75
  Epperson v. Arkansas, B: 51
  Frankfurter, Felix and, *B:* 69, 76–77
  Lockwood, Belva Ann and, *B:* 130
  Miranda, Ernest and, *B:* 150–51, 152
  Scottsboro Boys and, *B:* 165, 166, 168
  Sheppard, Sam and, *B:* 170, 174–75
  Warren, Earl and, *B:* 150
U.S. v. E.C. Knight Company
  PS: 140
USA Patriot Act
  A: 1: 51, 187–88; *2:* 253
  PS: 184, 206–7

V

Valenzuela, Carol
  B: 35

Valley State Prison for Women
  A: 2: 305 (ill.)
Vanzetti, Bartolomeo
  B: 72–76, 73 (ill.)
Verona, Roxana
  A: 1: 59
VICAP (Violent Criminal Apprehension Program)
  B: 123
Vice crime. *See* Moral offenses
Vices. *See also* Crimes
  B: 178–79
Victim and Witness Protection Act
  A: 2: 238–40
Victim Assistance Legal Organization
  A: 2: 241
Victim Rights Clarification Act
  A: 2: 238
Victimless crimes. *See also* Public order crimes
  PS: 78
Victims
  assistance programs, *A: 2:* 233–34
  bill of rights, *A: 2:* 236–38
  Black Americans, *A: 2:* 423–24
  colonial period, *A: 2:* 231–32
  compensation programs, *A: 2:* 234–35
  English common law, *A: 1:* 9
  Federal victims' rights legislation, *A: 2:* 238
  mediation, *A: 2:* 237
  murder, *A: 1:* 64
  protection, *A: 2:* 238–40
  rape, *A: 1:* 72–73
  right to sue, *A: 2:* 232–33
  rights of, *A: 2:* 235–38
  robbery, *A: 1:* 67
  role, *A: 2:* 242–43
  statistics, *A: 2:* 229
  studies of, *A: 2:* 241–43
  of Ted Bundy, *B:* 35
  victim advocates, *A: 2:* 240–41
  white-collar crime, *A: 1:* 94
Victims of Child Abuse Act
  A: 2: 238
Victims of Child Abuse Laws
  A: 2: 369
Victims of Crime Act (VOCA)
  A: 2: 235, 236

Victims of Trafficking and Violence Protection Act
A: 2: 366
Victims' Rights and Restitution
Act
A: 2: 238
Vietnam War
A: 1: 174–75; *2:* 329
Vigilantes
A: 1: 34–35; *2:* 249
Violence
black American communities,
A: 2: 424
drop in rates of, *A: 1:* 57
fear of, *A: 1:* 55
media, *A: 2:* 388
minority communities, *A: 2:*
432
motorcycle gangs, *A: 1:* 122
Native Americans, *A: 2:* 336–37
police and, *A: 2:* 256
rates of, *A: 1:* 53, 61
school, *B:* 111, 114–15, 116
women victims, *A: 2:* 232
Violence Against Women Act
A: 1: 73; *2:* 232, 297
Violent Crime Control and Law
Enforcement Act
A: 2: 238, 405
Violent Criminal Apprehension
Program (VICAP)
B: 123
Virginia, *PS:* 129
capital punishment, *A: 2:* 403
Declaration of Rights, *A: 1:* 22
(ill.)
settlement of, *A: 1:* 3–4, 7–8
Virginia Company
A: 1: 3–4, 7–8
PS: 3, 17, 26
Virginia Declaration of Rights
A: 1: 22 (ill.), 28
Viruses, computer
A: 1: 194
Visions and witchcraft
PS: 31
VOCA (Victims of Crime Act)
A: 2: 235, 236
Voiceprinting, forensic
B: 122
Volkswagen Bug, Bundy's, Ted
B: 32, 33, 34 (ill.)
Vollmer, August
A: 1: 43, 45; *2:* 255, 267

Volstead Act
A: 1: 38
Voluntary manslaughter
A: 1: 62–63
Volunteers in prisons
A: 2: 397 (ill.), 398
Voting. *See* Women's suffrage
Voyeurism
A: 1: 135

W

Wackenhut Corrections Corpo-
ration
A: 2: 310
Wall Street (Stone)
B: 23
Wall Street financiers
B: 17–23
Walling, George Washington
B: 184–91
Wal-Mart
A: 1: 162–63
Walnut Street Jail
A: 1: 30, 30 (ill.)
Wanted posters
B: 160
War. *See* specific wars
"War on drugs"
A: 1: 47; *2:* 310, 311 (ill.),
316, 426, 430–32
PS: 95
"War on Terror"
A: 1: 172, 184–85
PS: 203, 209, 210, 211
Warez groups
A: 1: 203
Warrants
A: 1: 27; *2:* 253
PS: 49, 51
Warren, Earl
A: 2: 259–60, 259 (ill.)
B: 57, 75, 150–51, 151 (ill.)
The Washing Away of Wrongs
(book)
A: 2: 266
Washington
PS: 116
Washington Post
B: 102
Washington, Raymond
A: 1: 125

Washington Research Project
A: 2: 370
Wastewater
A: 1: 166–67
Watchmen
A: 1: 14, 34; *2:* 246, 247 (ill.)
Water pollution
A: 1: 153–54, 153 (ill.)
Watts, C. L.
PS: 164, 166, 168
Watts race riots
A: 1: 124
Way of the Wiseguy (book)
A: 2: 446
Weapons. *See also* Firearms
aggravated assault, *A: 1:* 69
murder, *A: 1:* 64
robbery, *A: 1:* 68
and terrorism, *PS:* 211, 212,
223–25
Weather Underground
A: 1: 174–75
Weeks v. U.S.
A: 2: 260
Weems, Charles
B: 162, 169
PS: 160, 170, 171
Weinman, Carl
B: 174
Wells, Alice Stebbins
A: 1: 35, 37
Wells, Marcia. *See* Stanford, Sally
West, Thomas
PS: 19
Western Federation of Miners
(WFM)
B: 84
Western frontier
A: 2: 249
Wexler, Irving
B: 56–57
WFM (Western Federation of
Miners)
B: 84
What is to Be Done? (Cherny-
shevsky)
B: 80
Whipping
A: 1: 16, 19, 33
Whistle-stops
B: 58
White Slave Traffic Act
A: 1: 37, 42

White slavery
  B: 179
White supremacist groups
  A: 1: 175–76; *2:* 434 (ill.), 435
White-collar crime, *A: 1:* 93
    (ill.); *B:* 17–23
  causes, *A: 1:* 216–17
  cost of, *A: 2:* 412–13
  definition, *A: 1:* 52, 92
  environmental crime as, *A: 1:*
    151
  fraud, *A: 1:* 92, 94
  high-profile cases, *A: 1:* 52–53
  Microsoft settlement, *PS:*
    142–43
  motives, *A: 1:* 92
  organized crime, as distinct
    from, *PS:* 131, 133
  prosecution, *A: 1:* 94
  restraint of trade or com-
    merce, *PS:* 134
  shame penalties, *A: 2:* 395
  Sherman Antitrust Act, *PS:*
    136–37, 138–39, 140–45
  Standard Oil Company, *PS:*
    135, 136, 141
  trusts, *PS:* 135–36
  victims, *A: 1:* 94
Whoever Fights Monsters (Ressler)
  B: 123
Wickersham Commission
  A: 2: 411
Wickersham, George
  A: 1: 43; *2:* 254
  PS: 45, 67–75, 68 (ill.), 72
    (ill.)
Wilcox, Nancy
  B: 35
Williams, Abigail
  PS: 34–35, 36
Williams, Charles
  A: 2: 386
  PS: 166
Williams, Eugene
  B: 162, 166, 169
  PS: 161, 170 (ill.), 171
Williams, Jackie
  A: 1: 95 (ill.)
Williams, Jayson
  A: 2: 447
Wilson, Orlando W.
  A: 2: 256
Wilson, Woodrow
  B: 72, 89, 90, 132, 133

Wireless communications
  PS: 222–23
Wiretapping
  A: 1: 42
  PS: 191, 206, 207
Wirz, Henry, trial of
  A: 2: 325 (ill.)
Wisconsin
  A: 1: 31
Witchcraft
  A: 1: 10, 11 (ill.), 16, 18
Witch-hunts
  PS: 4, 29–40, 30 (ill.)
Witness protection programs
  A: 2: 238–40, 239 (ill.)
"The Wobblies"
  B: 84, 85
Women. *See also* specific women
  crime, effects of, *A: 2:* 416
  criminals, *A: 1:* 18
  education and, *B:* 3, 135–36
  law practice and, *B:* 130,
    135–37, 138–39
  police, *A: 1:* 35, 37
  prison, *A: 1:* 42; *2:* 316–17
  transporting across state lines,
    A: 1: 37, 42
  victims, *A: 2:* 232
  violence against, *B:* 33–36
Women's Christian Temperance
    Union
  PS: 98
Women's International League
    for Peace and Freedom
  B: 2–3, 7
Women's Peace Officers Associa-
    tion of California
  A: 1: 37
Women's Peace Party
  B: 2
Women's rights
  Anthony, Susan B. and, *B:*
    136
  Lockwood, Belva Ann and, *B:*
    129, 131
  Mansfield, Arabella and, *B:*
    134, 138–39
Women's suffrage, *B:* 131 (ill.),
    132
  Addams, Jane and, *B:* 2
  Anthony, Susan B. and, *B:*
    136–37
  Lockwood, Belva Ann and, *B:*
    129, 131, 132

Mansfield, Arabella and, *B:*
    134, 135, 139
  National Woman's Suffrage
    Association, *B:* 138 (ill.)
Wood, Catherine
  B: 41
Wood, Fernando
  B: 185–86, 187
Woodham, Luke
  A: 2: 383
Work release programs
  A: 2: 320
Workhouses
  A: 1: 18
Working Group on Unlawful
    Conduct Involving the Use
    of the Internet
  A: 1: 204
Workplaces
  A: 1: 157
World Trade Center
  A: 1: 51, 169 (ill.), 184
  PS: 185 (ill.), 198
World War I
  A: 2: 327
  B: 7, 54, 83, 85, 90
World War II
  childcare, *A: 2:* 361
  military justice, *A: 2:* 328
  military police, *A: 2:* 327
Worldcom
  A: 1: 52–53
Wright, Andrew
  B: 162, 169
  PS: 161, 166, 168, 170
Wright, Roy
  B: 162, 166, 169
  PS: 161, 162, 171
Writers
  B: 39–44, 61–68
Written laws
  A: 1: 28
Wurst, Andrew
  A: 2: 383

Y

Yeardley, Sir George
  PS: 26
Youth development centers
  A: 2: 351
Youth gangs. *See* Street gangs
Yugoslavia, former
  A: 2: 297

Z

Zantop, Susanne and Half
  A: 1: 59
Ze Wai Wong
  A: 1: 145
"Zero tolerance" policies
  A: 2: 390
  PS: 96
"Zoot suits"
  A: 1: 126, 127 (ill.)
Zuranski, Faith. *See* Kinkel, Faith